ENTREPRENEUR SHIP GRAVEYARD

Real-Life Success-To-Failure Business and Startup Stories

NEBOJSA "NESHA" TODOROVIC

CONTENTS

FAQ Your FAQs	1
Like Father Entrepreneur, Like Son Spendeur	3
C++ar Wash	11
Look And You Shall See: The Power of One Busy Little Bee!	20
Never Enough Money - My Entrepreneur Honey	30
My Neighbor - Steven Jobsky	39
Desperate StartupWives	46
Crazy, Stupid, Young Entrepreneur's Love	54
What's Up WhatsApp 2.0?	65
The Entrepreneur Who Would Be King	70
Blue Collar Entrepreneurs Blues	77
A Tale of Two Co-Founders	82
Entrepreneurs Alchemists and Money-Making Artists	90
The Startup Fountain of Youth	96
My Entrepreneur Amigo With A Big Ego	102
About The Author	109

FAQ YOUR FAQS

You: Are you an entrepreneur?
Me: Nope.

You: How many startups have you launched?
Me: None.

You: What are YOU doing here?
Me: Sharing real-life stories about successful entrepreneurs and startups that failed miserably and stupidly.

You: Where do your stories come from?
Me: From more than ten years of working as a freelance writer for countless entrepreneurs and startups.

You: Are these stories true?
Me: Just like in the movies. "The following story is based on actual events. The names, locations, and events have been changed for dramatic purposes."

You: Why are there no stories with happy endings?
Me: Buzz off!

You: Are all of your stories works of art?
Me: Yeah, absolutely!

You: Why have you been writing for losers only?
Me: Show some respect! Those aren't losers, but fighters who took a wrong turn.

You: Will your stories ruin my startup and entrepreneurship dreams?
Me: Don't become one of my stories, and you'll be just fine.

Entrepreneurship Is For Everyone But Not Everybody Can Be An Entrepreneur

LIKE FATHER ENTREPRENEUR, LIKE SON SPENDEUR

I respect all entrepreneurs, but I truly admire only the "founding fathers." The silver spooners don't impress me.

The Son hired me. For more than thirty years, The Father has been running a successful business with no website and social media. The good old word-of-mouth. The time for a full-scale digital business transformation was long overdue. The Father was aware but reluctant. The Son was enthusiastic and impatient.

As a freelance writer, I was a part of the big remote team of developers, designers, and social media experts. Money wasn't the problem. The expectations were high, and the working atmosphere was great.

The heir to his father's business throne was our project manager too. He was a positive tech-savvy person with a clear vision of what needed to be done. It was a no-stress-for-us and I want-to-impress situation for him. He was friendly and supportive. Good vibes everywhere.

I was more than happy. I caught myself a whale—hundreds of pages for a new website. We already talked about regular posts. What more could a freelance writer wish for?

The first couple of weeks were on steroids. The Son was available around the clock. He managed to talk to each team member daily despite the different time zones. We had weekly meetings to present our progress to the Father. The proud old school example was like a kid in a candy store. He just couldn't get enough of even the tiniest details. We could feel the happiness in his voice over Skype. More than our work, he was happy with his Son's ability to successfully lead a team. I could see "future" written all over his smiling face.

These weekly meetings lasted for hours, but nobody complained. The Father used every opportunity to take us all back in time. The stories about his company's history were fun and interesting to listen to. More than once, he made his Son blush. He was showing us old photos as if we were sitting next to him. The "founding father" was so humble, entertaining, and energetic that no one dared or even wished to interrupt him.

It was one of those moments in life when you don't bother yourself to think, what could possibly go wrong here?

The Big Trouble in Our Small Paradise

It wasn't too good to be true, and there were no red flags. But things changed. The Son wasn't as active as he used to be at the beginning. We didn't make a big deal out of it. Why?

Because we were all experienced freelancers. We knew the drill. We were even grateful for the change of our course. We had more than enough time to familiarize ourselves with the company's business. To have someone breathing down your neck every single day during this phase of work would be counterproductive. The Son was definitely not a control freak.

Then, our weekly meetings silently became monthly meetings. Pretty soon, our regular monthly meetings became irregular. We meet when we meet. We could tell that the Father wasn't thrilled about his Son's new meeting rules.

When all of us eventually met, we could wrap it up in less than an hour. The reason was obvious. The Father stopped being a talkative person. He didn't even want to ask questions. He just nodded from time to time. His silence wasn't deafening, but painful and unpleasant. The Son tried to lighten up the mood the best he could, but his Father stonewalled him the whole time.

Not so long ago, we couldn't wait to meet and hear the old man talking and laughing. Now, we felt relieved each time the Son postponed our meetings.

I, personally, couldn't find a reason to worry or panic. The new pages were delivered according to our initial plan and agreement. I was a lone freelance wolf in this story. The guys from the development, design, and social media teams were pros, but not particularly interested in making new friends. I began to wonder if they knew something I didn't at the time.

The last meeting was a turning point. For the first time, the Son didn't have anyone to present the results to. The Father was absent. We just didn't buy the Son's story that the old man wasn't feeling well. The irony was that the Son himself looked as if he just jumped out of the all-night party. Seeing him sitting in his Father's chair didn't feel right. We couldn't tell if he was more tired, embarrassed, frustrated, or all of these together.

The moment I hit the disconnect button felt as if someone just stabbed me in the stomach. I'm sure, I wasn't the only one feeling that way.

You Too, Brutus?!

My last payment didn't go through. I waited a couple of days, and then I emailed one of the guys from the design team. One-line answer. "Get on Skype asap!"

"We don't work on this website anymore. The Son found a new designer. Did you get paid?" That was too much to process for me at once. What's going on? Instead of the whole team, there's just one designer now?! They didn't get paid too?! Oh boy, this is worse than I thought.

It was a quick call with lots of "what" and "why" left unanswered. "What are you going to do? We are calling the Father because the Son is ignoring our calls and messages."

Well, I'm going to honor the chain of command. To my huge surprise, the Son answered right away. "Hey, what's up! How do you like my new car?"

The Son's phone camera was on. I was looking at some four-wheel beast from the Fast and Furious franchise. Wow! I was taking a deep breath to fire some questions, but he was quicker.

"I'm so glad you like it. Hey, don't worry about the payment. It's on its way." If a picture is worth a thousand words, I'm not sure how one breath into a phone's microphone counts. "It's so cool you aren't like those crazy designers. Can you imagine it, they called my Father? Yes, I could. As if money is the problem for me. No, it certainly is not."

Finally, he stopped babbling. I could see that he just discovered some new flashing button inside his car—my turn to talk.

"What happened to the designing team? Did they do something wrong?" I felt bad for even asking these ridiculous questions, but I wanted to get paid.

"Oh, my dear friend, you are the only one that understands me. It's not just them. I had to bring on new people for development and social media too." This time "wow" didn't cross my lips. "You're going to love working with those two new guys, I've found. Trust me."

My head was killing me. The whole team is reduced to just one man. So, instead of three teams, we now had three people.

"It's much cheaper this way, and we will be more efficient. Most of the work has already been done. We just need a few finishing touches." I wanted to say something, but then I remembered, I had to get paid. Based on the number of remaining pages that needed content, I would say that we were light-years away from "a few finishing touches."

I just had enough of him for one day. Luckily for me, his mind was already somewhere else.

"Sorry buddy, I have to go. I just realized that I like a model with a panoramic roof more. I'm gone. This thing is wild." I was still holding a phone when he hung up. I'm sure that my face would've been a great meme.

I wandered for a moment. Was I next? Was he going to replace me too? The fact that I was a one-man team calmed me down. My story about the prodigal son wasn't over, though.

Sad But True - The Call Out Of The Blue

Here we were. The three musketeers and I, the digital D'Artagnan, with Livin-La-Vida-Loca-Son. Yup, loca, loca situation. When you don't have much of a choice, the best thing you can do is to mind your own business. That's exactly what we all did. The Son was resurfacing every now and then from the ocean of wild nightlife to give us working instructions and take care of late payments. Eventually, we reached a point where he'd just say, you know what to do. Then, he'd be MIA again, for weeks.

I'd been working on more than one project at the time, but I just couldn't wait to get rid of this one, officially. The last page, the last payment, and I'd be gone. I already prepared a little "Dear John" speech in my head to avoid writing a blog. The website was like, you know that famously infamous "unfinished horse drawing" meme. Google it, just in case you don't know what I'm talking about.

We had a strong and promising start according to the original plan. Then, we turned the beautiful work of the previous teams into a grotesque compromise. Trust me, it was painful to watch.

Quite a few features were missing, and social media buttons were the roads to nowhere. I couldn't afford to worry about someone else's problems. Write. Deliver. Hunt a young wannabe entrepreneur to get paid. Repeat.

I remember how much time, cigarettes, and irregular heartbeats took me to teach my folks, especially my father, how to use Skype. So, you can imagine my surprise when I saw that the Father was calling me. I didn't know what to say. I didn't answer the first call. But, I just couldn't ignore the second one.

My apology and "explanation" were ready, but I didn't have the time to use them. You can't make a fool out of the old school.

"It's OK, my son. You're all my kids. There's no reason for you to feel uncomfortable. You did nothing wrong here. I know what's going on. It hasn't been the first time for my only son to let me down. I already called all of you, every single one of you, both old and new kids. You're my last call."

I did my best that the Father didn't hear me breathing. I felt so grateful that his camera wasn't turned on. That would be just too much to bear. I'm not going to lie and say that I cried, but it was painful to listen to the old man's voice. I could feel the strength and pride in his words that were hammering me down.

"Did you get paid? Do we." he said we, not he or my Son, "owe you something for your work?"

"No, no, Sir. Everything is OK. We had some," I wanted to say problems, but instead, I used. "Hiccups. Now, everything is OK."

"Good. Good. That's good to hear." I thought that we were done with our conversation. He was cleaning after his Son, and I just wanted to get over it, being the last name on the Father's call list.

"I didn't ask this, any of you guys. What did I do wrong?" People like to confess to writers, don't they? I mean, kudos to my colleagues: freelance developers, designers, and other nocturnal digital creatures, but the matters of a broken heart are under the writers' jurisdiction. I started my business-from-nothing story. You know all there is to it.

I felt like I'm in the Horrible Bosses movie - part one, just to be clear. It wouldn't be fair to compare the Son with the "Tool" portrait by Colin Farell. Also, the Father and I never had a chance to develop that kind of relationship Donald Sutherland and Jason Bateman showed in the movie. It's a horrible comparison to bring the Horrible Bosses into this story, but go see the movie, if you haven't already, and then, feel free to judge me.

"You're a good man, Sir. I'm a father too. I want my kid to live a better life than me. That's something my father told me. It's our duty to ensure better lives for the next generation. That's the problem too. We have different starting points. Each new generation takes the achievements of the previous one for granted. But, you did your duty. You should feel good about it. Your Son is young. This is just a phase. It will pass, much sooner than later. He'll be on the right track before you know it. This will be a lesson to him."

"Thank you, my dear son. Thank you so much. God bless you, your father, and your kid." I said nothing. The black screen. There's the second part of my comforting story, I kept to myself. If something or someone (the Son) doesn't change quickly and dramatically, thirty years-long business legacy will be gone in less than three years.

Successful entrepreneurs may be the kings, but the succession to their business thrones doesn't always turn out as planned and desired. Blood is thicker than water. Well, maybe this one can be applied to someone else, but not to the entrepreneurs.
So, now you know why I respect the kids, but I only admire - the founding fathers.

There's an abyss between my professional respect and my personal admiration. It's bottomless for a reason.

An Entrepreneur Without At Least One Nervous Breakdown Is Just Like A Warrior Without Any Battle Scars

C++AR WASH

Have you heard about the "COVID20+" rule? I have to thank my remote friends for it. What's it all about?

Well, it's about tips. How much money do you usually tip? We are all somewhere in the tip zone between 10% and 20%, aren't we? Because of this whole pandemic thing, there's an unofficial initiative to leave more than 20% tips. There's no need to ask "why," I hope. Support your local economy. I'm addressing my remote work fellows all over the world. Leave as much as you can.

Let's show some solidarity. Not all people can work remotely. And, that's not the only reason. Without your local restaurants, gyms, shops, and all other big and small things and services you can imagine and need, your remote work (life) loses its meaning. Am I right?

Don't be stingy as a general rule, and especially now during the pandemic. OK?

I preach what I teach and put my money where my mouth is with the guys who work at a local car wash. Just to be clear, I'm not driving something you have never seen before. On the contrary, my car is older than my teenage kid. Furthermore, my car is officially the ugliest one in the world. I'm talking about Fiat Multipla.

You can Google it and see for yourself. Make sure you're looking at the older models with the nicknames, such as "alien" or "froggy." The journalists at "The Sunday Times" were merciless when comparing my car to the Elephant Man in 2018.

I don't take it personally. I don't mind. My Fiat Multipla serves multiple purposes. One of the most important ones for me has nothing to do with driving. Here's the thing.

I have a soft spot for street dogs. I don't like to call them stray dogs. For me, they're freelancers of the animal kingdom. I mean no disrespect, and please, don't take this the wrong way. This is where I stand, very personally. I look at all those street dogs, and I see myself. A street dog without a home is like a freelancer without a regular job. You go from one place to another, or in my case, from one project to another. You hope that a long-term client will adopt you eventually. My comparison is wrong on so many levels, and it's OK if you don't like it. But, if you're offended by it regardless of the reasons, then you're heartless, period. Moving on with my story.

Because of a street dog that sleeps in my car, I have to visit my local car wash friends quite more often than usual. I can't adopt this street dog because my French poodle Fifi is an old lady with a nasty temper when it comes to territorial disputes. I built with my own hands or paid for three dog houses. All of them were demolished or removed promptly and officially. Some of the neighbors of my apartment complex aren't dog-friendly.

Especially when it comes to the street gods. Now, you get the picture.

So, every winter, my car transforms into a comfy five-star dog house, but only from dusk till dawn. I kid you not, every single winter night for the last couple of years. I'm not complaining; I'm just explaining my situation. This is where my Fiat Multipla comes in handy like no other car in the world. This car has two rows of three seats, both front, and back. So, this isn't a "traditional" five-seater car. So what, one may ask.

The first row of seats serves as the "wall" or barrier in my car. My four-legged night guest likes to sleep on the first row of seats. If it hadn't been for this wall of the first row seats, the street dog would have slept on a different seat every night. This would drive my Fifi crazy that treats the back seats as the extended exclusive territory of our apartment. No, I'm not going to make any comparisons when it comes to this one. You got the idea by now. I use more than one warm blanket during one winter season. When you have a street dog sleeping in your car every night, you have to get up before sunrise. This can be tricky.

If I'm opening my car's door too soon, I have to deal with those heartbreaking sleeping eyes. It's even worse than that famous Puss in Boots sad-looking eyes. If I'm too late, the street dog does her best to be patient, but she often has to use my car as a bathroom. My bad. I was too late.

During the summers, I don't have these problems. She likes to sleep outside, and there's no way you can get her into a car when it's lovely weather outside. When it's cold and windy with rain or snow, I don't even have to bother to check because she's already waiting for me next to my car.

This street dog is a sweetheart. She's so smart and respectful. But, when I'm late, nature calls, and she does what she has to do. That's why I always have more than one blanket in my car. Plus, I have to drive to a car wash after each "incident," if I want to avoid my wife's rolling eyes and Fifi's cartoonish behavior. I'm not getting into this car. You know, the dogs' thing when it comes to the different scents.
Now, you get it, what's the reason I'm more than just a regular customer of our local car wash.

The guys working there are super friendly and full of understanding, including the owner himself. I get discounts by default.

Luckily for me, that's not an ordinary car wash because they are into the interior cleaning business, among other things. So, all my blankets and car seats get the top-class cleaning treatment. While one blanket is drying, I always have one in reserve because I can't allow my street dog to spend a night on the street.

I'm grateful for the special treatment my car wash team is giving me. In return, I'm more than generous with my tips. While I'm waiting for my car to be cleaned, I keep hearing the horror stories about people who should be ashamed of the street dog sleeping in my car when it comes to the things you leave behind and personal hygiene. This street dog feels guilty about it, at least. She's avoiding me the whole day when she does something "wrong" in my car. In the early evening, she's already waiting for me to let her in. I'm not mad, and I will never be.

My word of advice, respect the guys who're washing your car. Why? Well, one of the reasons is, you never know who you're talking to.

A Computer Genius With A Sponge and Hose

I remember that I left a five-dollar tip. The car wash took the money and looked at the bills with a hard to describe look. "I used to make five hundred a day." His smile was a mixture of bitterness and sadness.

I reached out to my wallet to give more. "No, no, it's OK buddy, I meant no disrespect. I was just talking to myself. Compared to all of our clients, you're the most generous and regular one. I'm sorry. See you next time."

I didn't feel right. I knew there was more to it than this.

"Hey, about a round of beer after you finish your shift? I will come to pick you up." He was looking through me. There was no anger in his eyes, just the bottomless sadness of some buried memory I triggered with my tip. "Please. Don't make me ask twice. Just want to talk." He was squeezing a sponge and hosing down a car wash driveway. Still not a word. "Please."

"OK, but no need to pick me up. Wait for me in the coffee shop at the mall. I can walk there." I wanted to offer a ride one more time, but I stayed silent. I was grateful that he accepted my invitation. I didn't want to push him any further.

"Great. I'll be waiting for you."

While I was driving, it struck me. I offered beer, and he wanted to meet at the coffee shop. Can we get beer there? Oh, it doesn't matter. I just want to talk to the guy.

He was always nice to me. I owe him so much more than professional courtesy. He likes dogs too. He told me that more than once. Something happened today. I wasn't sure what and why exactly. Was it something I said, did, or gave? It couldn't be about the money. Sometimes I give more. Sometimes I give less. But, I never drive to a car wash unless I have money for a tip.

"You still haven't ordered?" The car wash guy surprised me. I didn't see him entering the coffee shop.

"No, I was waiting for you." I was about to ask what we should order.

"I don't drink alcohol. I can't. It's because of my meds." He sat down with the hands firmly on his knees. "I stopped smoking too. I had to." His last line caught me with a cigarette in my mouth. I was about to put it out, but he stopped me.

"It's OK, it doesn't bother me. I know that coffee without a cigarette sucks, but can you make a sacrifice for me, please?" He actually smiled for a change.

"Sure. Absolutely." I was so relieved. Maybe this time, we would get it on the right foot.

Two coffees were on their way to our table. I took a deep breath to explain myself today, but there was no need for that. The car wash guy took care of it.

"I told you, it's OK. Relax. It has nothing to do with you. I heard that you are a freelancer. Right?" I nodded."A developer? A designer?" I had that stupid look on my face as if I were sorry for disappointing him. "A writer then. That's cool too. I always wanted to write."

I said that I always wanted to learn how to code. We both laughed. It felt good. We were both relaxed.

"You know, I used to work on databases for big banks. I traveled a lot. Every night in a different hotel. All costs covered. First-class flights. Before all of this." Oh no, another collateral pandemic victim. He was determined to do all the talking that night. "It had nothing to do with COVID. I also used to have my own software company back in the days. More than ten people." I had a series of silent wows. Who was this guy? What's doing in a car wash now?

"Things went crazy. I wanted to keep up. I really tried. I couldn't remember when I had a good night's sleep. First, the energy drinks kept me going on. Then, I had to switch to the pills." I needed a cigarette. I didn't ask for his approval. I didn't apologize. "One day, I just lost it. I passed out. They said that they found me on the bathroom floor in a hotel. They had to scan my head. Something snapped inside. My doctor told me that I can go on like this and dig my own grave or just stop."

I looked the other way, "As if it is for your doctor to say."

"Actually, it wasn't. He is my brother-in-law. My wife was pregnant with our first child then." I was worried that I wouldn't have enough cigarettes to help me get through his story by the time we were done with our coffees. "My wife's parents own the car wash. So, you see, it's not all that bad. I enjoy what I'm doing right now. I turn on some nice music, and I shut myself off completely. The most important thing is not to worry and stay away from computers. I don't watch TV. I don't even have a phone. My former clients are still trying to get in touch with me, but my wife is one hell of a firewall."

We laughed, but I was somewhere else. I tried to imagine how he must have felt. I gave up immediately. My head hurt. I closed my eyes for a moment. I was pressing my hands against my forehead.

"Do you have headaches too? Do you take anything?"

I hesitated, but then I realized, it was pointless not to talk about it. "Not so often, but I can't get through a single day without cigars and tranquilizers. It's a mission impossible for me." He said nothing.

AC/DC "Highway to Hell" was playing in the background. What an appropriate music theme for this lovely and inspirational conversation. Am I going to end up just like him? Am I on my highway to cyber hell? Had he bitten more than he could chew back then?

"Do you need a ride back home?"
"No, I will walk. I have to walk. It's good for my health." There was irony in his voice when he said that. "You know, my doctor's orders."

"Yeah, I know." When was the last time I went to see mine? I kept the last question to myself.

Choose! What Do You Have To Lose? Except for Everything.

The last time I saw my cyber-car-was-friend was on a hot summer day. The ideal time for the deep cleaning of my car's first-row seats. The weather has to be perfect for seats to dry in the sun properly. I came to pick up my car a bit earlier than I was told.

It seemed that a former rocket-scientist coder had a family day at work. I saw two small kids who had their win-win day. They were helping their dad to wash cars and using every opportunity to play their water games with hoses. I stopped and just looked at them. I didn't want to ruin the moment.

There was a young woman who was helping them. My guess, the mother of those kids and his wife because I hadn't seen her before.

"C'mon, boys! Enough is enough. You had your fun. Time to get into the house and put on dry clothes." His wife crossed her arms on her chest. No word of approval from her. "C'mon, guys, the water is ice cold. You're going to get sick or something." He was exaggerating, but how could you possibly blame him? I sure did not.

"It is better for them to catch a cold than to cry their eyes out playing video games all day long." The wife grabbed the kids and left before they could even realize what was going on. The car wash guy squeezed sponges in his hands, dead dry. He dropped and started rubbing the back of his head. My wife has the same effect on me. When she is up to it, she knows how to make my head explode.

What I witnessed was obviously something different and much deeper than a "typical" marriage fight.

That woman was determined to keep their kids away from the shiny screens of the tempting digital world. I had no doubts about it. Those kids won't follow their father's digital footsteps. The mother will make sure of it, this way or another.

I turned back and left without him seeing me. I had the whole day to pick up my car. The front row seats will be wet and unusable for a considerable time. I knew all of that, but I wanted to pay the car wash guy before he finished his shift. Remember? It was all about a tip. Damn the tips. What about life?

If It Makes Money It Ain't Funny

LOOK AND YOU SHALL SEE: THE POWER OF ONE BUSY LITTLE BEE!

Three friends. Three years and thirty beers later. We were happy and drunk. We had a legit reason to celebrate. One of us just got back to our hometown from a three-year-long work-and-work adventure in Germany. All those empty beer cans helped us confirm that Einstein was right. Time was relative. For us, who stayed at home, three years were like three minutes. We couldn't say the same for our Gastarbeiter friend.

For three years, he was in the work-eat-sleep-repeat mode. The company covered only the basic expenses and working visa costs. Food and free time activities not included. He was the finest example of the Spartan lifestyle you can possibly imagine. He was cutting corners to the extreme, so he could save as much money as possible. Not a single working holiday. No pause button. Nada.

Now, he's back, and he has a plan.

The two of us, "locals," were eager to hear what our busy friend plans to do with all that money. I mean, it isn't enough for him to retire, but it is just enough to change his life. That was his plan all along. Work hard. Invest smart. Enjoy later.

Our friend had three years to examine every single business and investment opportunity he could possibly think of. Time for his moment of business truth. What's his next move?

Business Ideas Are Like Opinions
- Everyone Has One

"I'm going to find and buy an old big house in a nice location. Then, I'm going to throw some money at it to make it shine like new. Then, I'm going to sell it or rent apartments. I had three years to learn all there's to know about construction work. I know where I can save money. I'm going to start small this year, but I plan to have more than one construction site next year." He shared his "master plan" with us, and then he started looking for a waitress to get us another round.

I didn't say this, but I really wanted to. Wow! Is this the best you can come up with? Wow! I looked at my other friend. He was far from being impressed too. What an epic disappointment. Yet, we had to put on our best fake smiles and nod like crazy.
Our Gastarbeiter friend was too drunk to see through us. I thought that was it. He's back. We packed three years we hadn't seen each other in three hours. Now, it's time to hit the road and get back to our lives. My other friend had a different plan. Actually, he had an idea.

"Hey, I have a better idea. Do you want to hear it?" He wasn't looking at me. I didn't mind. His idea was looking for a nest made of Euros to lay profit eggs.

The Gastarbeiter friend was like Leonardo DiCaprio in "Django Unchained." You know that line about curiosity and attention. I was all ears.

"What do you think about bee houses? Handmade. 100% natural materials. Fully EU certified, from A to Z."

Just like in the movies. There was a moment of silence, and then our Gastarbeiter friend transformed from Leonardo DiCaprio into Ray Liotta in "GoodFellas." He laughed so hard that he almost fell out of his chair, literally.

"Bee houses?! You have to be kidding me! You can't be serious about it. The Bee-man!" He wanted me to join his laughing party, but I found a way to keep my neutrality. A new round of beer was just on time.

The Bee-man friend couldn't take this joke at all. "I don't remember me laughing and ridiculing your "brilliant" idea. I thought we were friends. Why do you have to be like this?"

"Why did you want to share your bee house idea? I know. You need the money. You want me to invest my money into your stupid idea." The Gastarbeiter friend was looking at his Bee-man friend like a prosecutor. Admit that you are guilty. Admit it.

"Yes, I need the money. I thought, you could help. We would've split the profit. You don't have to lift a finger. I'd do all the work and take care of everything."

The Gastarbeiter friend was no longer a nice guy. "From the moment I came back, this is what you have been doing to me. Flying around me like your stupid bees asking for money to invest in your stupid ideas. I thought, my friend, that at least you are different. I thought that you'd be glad to see me."

"But, I am. I couldn't wait to see you again. I wouldn't have said a word about my idea, if you hadn't talked first about your reconstruction nonsense. Do you know how many people in our town, in this country, are trying and doing the same on a scale you can only dream about? And, talking about stupid ideas, my idea may be stupid, but it is original."

The Bee-man friend got up. The anger got him sober in a second. He was throwing the bills out of his wallet all over the table without thinking. I put my hand on his shoulder.

"C'mon, man. Let's all cool off. Let's order another round. This one is on me."

"Let me go! I'm done here." Our Bee-man was gone.

I looked at my Gastarbeiter friend. "What? Am I supposed to apologize? Is this what you want from me?"

I looked the other way. "No, I'm trying to understand. You crossed the line. You hurt his feelings."

"What about my feelings? I'm not an ATM! It's interesting how people reason here. They all have ideas, but when the moment comes to put the money where your mouth is, then you don't have much to say. Do you know why? Talk is cheap. Ideas are free. If you think that your idea is good and mine sucks, then don't ask for my money."

He was up to. Our reunion party was officially over. I reached out to my pocket to get my wallet. The Gastarbeiter friend grabbed my hand.

"I called you. I was so happy to see you again after all those years. You were my best friends. This is all on me. Take our friend's money and give it back to him. He will need it for his stupid bee houses. While he's building toy houses for bugs, I will be building real houses for real people."

He left without saying bye or even looking back. I was alone looking at the table full of empty beer cans and business ideas.

"How about another one?" I looked up at a waitress hovering over me with a smile from ear to ear.

"No, I'm good. Actually, I'm not good at all."

She gave me that look, oh, you stupid drunk man. I felt ashamed. I couldn't wait to get out and catch some fresh air.

Five Years Later - Time To Check Your Success Metter

Since that night, we had moved on with our lives. Here and there, we'd bump into each other. We were polite and cold. Very similar to the ex-couples who mastered the art of avoiding unpleasant topics.

My hands and conscience were clean. I didn't take sides. Yet, it was clear. Our friendship magic was gone. I had a life to live. Some of us got married and had kids. For me, that night became one unpleasant episode. For my friends, it would turn out to be one of the most important moments in their lives.

I had to deal with numbers and banks, so my wife could enjoy our first apartment hunt. We skipped agencies and went straight for property owners.

I was a bit surprised but not shocked to find out we were talking to a guy who was taking care of both renting and selling apartments in a dozen locations all over the city. He wasn't the owner. He was hired to deal with these things, so the owner, who's also his boss, doesn't have to. I was curious. Who's the person behind all these buildings? Usually, the people in this industry don't miss every single opportunity to advertise aggressively.

My wife was occupied with the feng shui aspect of our future family nest. I could see that the manager was grateful she didn't ask too many questions. I had one.

"How come I've never even heard of you?"

The manager wasn't surprised at all.

"We get that a lot from our tenants and buyers. The construction company I used to work for was taken over a few years ago by another company. Our new owner isn't into the construction business; this is one of his many enterprises."

I raised my eyebrows, which made the manager feel uncomfortable.

"Don't worry, my friend. We're just talking. I lost count of how many apartments we have checked this week. You know what I mean." He nodded with a huge smile and a feeling of relief.

"It's actually an interesting story. My first boss and the original owner started and unfortunately ended his construction business with just one reconstructed house."

I needed some additional info to make sure that isn't my Gastarbeiter friend, by any chance. I mean, what are the odds?

"What went wrong?"

The manager quickly checked what my wife was doing. She's admiring the view from a terrace.

"Where were we? Ah, yes. In my opinion, more than one factor. Our real estate market was already oversaturated. Plus, my old boss was obsessed with the idea of applying what he called the "German model" here."

Yup, that's my friend he's talking about. But, I needed to play along. "What do you mean? I don't get you?"

"Well, his priority was on renting, not on selling the apartments. He kept telling us that for most people in Germany, ownership isn't such a big deal. You know how our people are." He looked at my wife and me. He was telling the truth. "The whole of Eastern Europe was like that. In the name of sacred property ownership, we are ready to give up on many things. The folks from Western Europe like to travel, drive nice cars, and rely on building managers as tenants."

"Who eventually took over your company and the first building?"

"That's the most interesting part of my story."

You don't say. So, don't keep me waiting. I was looking over my shoulder to make it clear that my wife could take away his patient listener at the worst possible moment for his story.

"You won't believe it, but I swear to you, what I'm telling is true. A guy who makes bee houses cashed my old boss out as if it's nothing. Can you believe it?"

Actually, I can. "Sorry, we really have to go. Honey, wrap it up, please. I have to visit an old friend."

You Have Been A Busy Little Bee, Haven't You?

I was examining a model of a bee house when my Bee-man friend stepped into his office.

"Oh, look what the cat dragged in! I couldn't believe it when my secretary told me your name. Sorry for keeping you waiting, buddy. I got stuck in the production." We hugged and looked at what the time did to us. We laughed. It felt good. "Sit down. Relax. My secretary will get us something to drink in no time."

"No need, really. I see you're busy. I don't want to take your time." It seemed that I unintentionally changed the course of what was supposed to be an honest, friendly welcome.

"Do you need anything? Don't tell me that you're thinking about making honey?" I wanted to spice "no" with a smile, but the damage was already done. "Just spit it out. What is it that you need?"

Maybe there's still a way to soften the situation. "My wife and I are thinking about buying one of your apartments."

He blushed with embarrassment. "Why don't you say so? I will get you a discount." I was able to quickly mention the bank. "Forget about the banks. You don't need that. Move-in right away and pay when and how much you want. I don't care. You're my friend."

"Thank you so much. I can't tell you how much this means to my wife and me. Can I just ask you one more thing? But please, don't take it the wrong way. Please. I needed to know what happened to our mutual friend."

He just nodded and looked me in the eye. He didn't want to hide his disappointment. Now, it was my turn to feel embarrassed.

What happened to our Gastarbeiter friend? The Bee-man took a deep breath before answering.

"He went back to Germany. I haven't heard from him since the takeover. Did he send you here?"

"No, no, absolutely no. I also haven't heard from him in years. I had nothing to do with your thing. Remember? Your business ideas. I couldn't care less. You're both my friends."

"Yeah, I'll give you that. That's the only reason I'm not throwing you out of my office now."

I didn't want to leave him with a bad taste in my mouth. "Hey, just forgot about all of it. Tell me about this business miracle of yours. That's a story I want to hear."

The Bee-man lightened up. He already pressed a button. "Please bring a bottle, you know which one, and two glasses. You, sit down behind my desk and make yourself comfortable."

The Bee-man was walking around his huge office with a glass in his hand. He stopped from time to time only to point at some of the many pictures on his office wall.

"So, you see, my friend. If it makes money, it ain't funny."

"I never said that."

He just couldn't let it go. "I know, I know, but our friend thought it was funny. I just signed a new contract. I will be supplying the whole Scandinavian market now. How about that?"

"Wait, I don't get it. No disrespect to you, my friend. Don't they know how to make bee houses themselves?"

"Yes, they do, but they just can't make enough. And, even if they could meet the demand, they would still buy from me because it's cheaper. You see, my friend, they care more about the bees than we do."

"But, what about the competition? You aren't the only one in the world to make bee houses, are you?"

"True, but I spent tons of money on all the certificates you can possibly think of. This office is too small for all of them. Do you think it's cheap to make environment-friendly products to the tiniest detail and the last requirement? But, I did my math. I started right on time. I'm playing by the book. And, it's working for me."

"Yeah, I can see that. And, what about your construction business? I also heard you don't keep your hands in the honeypot, only."

The Bee-man laughed. "I have to take care of my family. My brother-in-law is running the construction division of my company. My wife is doing something with cosmetic products. I don't even know what that's all about. But, bee houses are my business babies, and mine alone. This is how it all started. This is how all other businesses started. Thanks to one little bee that bit when I was just a kid. Do you know that a bee bites only once?"

"Yes, I know."

"It's the same in business and friendship. Focus on just one business idea, and make it count. And, don't bite your friends. Get up. Let me show you around."

True Entrepreneurship Is The Kingdom of Conscience Or Something Else That Has Nothing or Little To Do With It

NEVER ENOUGH MONEY - MY ENTREPRENEUR HONEY

"Look, my friend, here's the thing. I can't afford to be a controversial writer. I even got an award for the most controversial writer of the year. OK? You, on the other hand, can't afford to be a controversial businessman. Not even for a minute. There's no award for it."

Can you believe it? I actually said that to one of my clients and the antihero of this story. I'm going to call him - Baby.

No worries. Breaking Bad and Narcos are my favorite TV shows. Ah, wait. It wouldn't be unfair not to mention Peaky Blinders. But, that's it. I can. I know how and when to draw a line between fiction and reality. Could Baby say the same? I don't know. I don't care.

There's no thin line between morality and profitability. My Baby snorted his line somewhere along the way. This is his story.

Per Aspera Ad Opel Astra

Baby was born at an interesting time. While Germans were celebrating the fall of the Berlin Wall, his parents were celebrating his first birthday.

Baby didn't like school. As soon as he finished elementary school, he earned his first money. Then, right after the EU opened its door to Eastern Europe, he was old enough to get a passport. Pet Shop Boys' song "Go West" was about something else, but for Baby was a clear sign of where to move next.

He was importing used cars to his home country. His countrymen wanted to drive better cars. They couldn't afford the new ones. So, this was a win-win scenario for Baby and his family and friends, who were his first buyers.

Baby had to deliver the first "shipment" himself driving back and forth one used car at the time. Pretty soon, he had enough money to pay for a car transport truck. The next thing you know, he was coordinating a small, but an efficient fleet of these trucks.

I know what you're thinking. Ha! What's the big deal? Anybody can do it. That's not entirely true because there's a catch.

First, you need to find used cars that you can buy cheap in the West and sell dear in the East. Meaning, you have to make connections with the sellers of used cars.

Then, you have to make connections with the car repair shops in your home country. I'm talking about a network of auto mechanics that can justify your price with their repairs.

Finally, you have to build a network of used car salesmen that will work for you. There's no way you can make this story of selling used cars from one side of Europe to the other short and simple.

Every single used car had to be "processed" individually. Let's not forget the customs and all paperwork associated with it.

Baby knew how to drive through the jungle of used car dealers, car mechanics, custom officials, and buyers. He reached a stage when he used to spend all of his time behind a computer and on the phone instead of behind the wheel and in countless car repair shops. His business was flying in autopilot mode. Baby just had to make sure that his key people were always at the right time and in the right places.

The wheels were running smoothly. The years were passing quickly. There was work available for all of his family members and friends. His parents were living in a new big house. His wife was his right-hand man. His kids were attending the most expensive private schools. They were traveling, building, and buying with no need to worry about how much they were spending. Life was good for Baby.

That was the moment when Baby decided to contact me.

I Am Off The Hook - Write Me A Book

I didn't buy a car from Baby, if that's what you're thinking. He bought me with his version of from rags to riches story. He needed a ghostwriter to write a book about his life. I was up for it. His story was worth writing and sharing—no question about it.

We officially met for the first time on St. Petka's Day in his luxurious home. One of many he owned. I remember that it was a hot day in October. It felt almost like summer. Until that day, we exchanged a couple of emails and spoke a few times over the phone. My freelance friend who designed his company's website recommended me.

This day had a special meaning for him. On that day, he fell asleep behind the wheel and almost got killed. He managed to regain control of a car just in time to stay on the highway. That was one of the first cars he had to drive and sell himself. Those days were behind him, but the memory was obviously still alive. He was grateful. That's why he decided to celebrate this particular day as his second birthday.

I got the point. He wanted to make sure that I don't take his business and success for granted, which I didn't. The story itself was scary enough.

It was more than just a "birthday" party. Let me put it this way. Imagine that you are invited to the US embassy on the 4th of July. Can you get the picture now? It was crowded and noisy. The Great Gatsby would take notes and envy Baby. I'm not exaggerating. If only all of my clients were like Baby. That was one hell of a way to introduce yourself to your future biographer.

Our plan was simple. I was to interview him and write book chapters based on my notes. That was the beauty of it. Each chapter meant a different location. Baby was more than generous and super friendly.

He was reviving his business past most luxuriously. We were traveling and enjoying ourselves like never before in my life. Each time I finished and delivered a chapter was a call to party.

I didn't want to look like I was taking advantage of the situation. But Baby wouldn't take no for an excuse, not to "mark" a new book chapter in his own special way. He loved what I wrote about him and his business journey. He wanted me to get the right "feeling" of how it used to be for him back in the days.

The only challenge was to make sure I was writing sober. It was a mission impossible to keep up with Baby when he was in his party mode.

The best thing about the book, we were working together on, was his motivation. There was no room for the word "vanity" in his business dictionary. He didn't want to impress the world. He just wanted to leave something to his kids. I understood, respected, and admired his vision. The money doesn't grow on trees. That was the only and main message of his book. Baby had no plans for his kids to inherit his business. He was determined to give them the freedom to choose what they want to be and do in their lives.

He didn't want to be worshiped or idolized. Baby had a simple philosophy that covered both his business and life.

"I don't care what my kids or their kids are going to do with all I built and earned once I'm gone. I can't take money to my grave, so why should I worry about all of these? I'm always on the road. I don't have time to tell stories. Yet, I want my story to be told. My kids of all people should know it and understand it. Do you agree?"

"Absolutely! You're a good man, Baby. I love working for you. Your story deserves to be written. I will write my heart out for you."

"Let's get something to drink." That was Baby's way of showing that I found the right words.

What's With The Picture of Al Pacino, Mi Padrino?

For the last chapter of our book and the first chapter of his life, Baby took me to his small village where he grew up.

"Would you mind if we make a quick stop here first?"

My smile was my approval. I followed him to a small grocery store. The small group of villagers sitting on improvised chairs in front of the store greeted him like a hero. Everyone wanted to shake his hand.

"Give it to me." Baby was talking to a young girl that was working in a grocery store. "Beer for everyone you can find outside."

"Sure thing, Baby. Right away." She quickly handed him a small notebook with old and worn-out black covers. Before we knew it, she was gone. We were alone in a store. Baby spent a couple of minutes examining the content of the black notebook.

"Do you know what this is?" He touched my shoulder with the notebook.

"I have no idea."

Baby put the notebook next to the store's cash register. "Every small village has one. We call it the "black book of debts." I grew up looking at one every single day." He pulled the money out of his wallet and put it under the notebook. "Almost every family in our village has a page in this notebook. They come here and take what they need every day. You buy without money, and you leave your signature next to the amount and the date. Then, at the end of the month, they pay what they owe. No matter how careful and humble you are, there's always some money left to be paid. Whenever I come to visit my parents, I take care of it for the whole village."

"Don't you worry that some people may take advantage of the situation?"

Baby did his best to hide the bitterness and disappointment in his voice. "My people may be poor, but they're honest, hard-working, and above all honest to the bone."

"I'm so sorry, Baby. I didn't mean to…"

"It's OK. Forget about it." Let's go. My parents are waiting for us already. No restaurant can match my mother's cooking. He couldn't take his hand off the car's horn all the way to his parent's house.

You know what happened next. There were lots of hugs, kisses, and a few tears here and there. "Enough" was a forbidden word at his family's dining table. I felt as if I was going to explode at any moment.

"Let me show you where my old room used to be before we renovated the house. I was able to save only a few things. You know how it goes."

I nodded in approval. Then, one old picture caught my attention. It was the famously infamous Tony Montana's desk from the "Scarface" movie. The picture was old, but the frame was new. I gave Baby my WTH look.

"Hey, don't look at me like that." Baby laughed while throwing friendly and painless punches to my shoulder. "It's just a movie. I was just a kid. You don't think that Tony was my role model, do you?"

"Of course not. I'm just saying, of all the movie pictures, you picked this one where Al Pacino is sitting behind that desk. You know, it doesn't feel right for someone like you."

"I know, but hey, there's no successful business without at least a little bit of controversy. Right?"

Back to the very beginning of this story. One more time. I really said that, straight to his face.

"Look, my friend, here's the thing. I can't afford to be a controversial writer. I even got an award for the most controversial writer of the year. OK? You, on the other hand, can't afford to be a controversial businessman. Not even for a minute. There's no award for it."

I just landed on the dark side of Baby's business moon without even realizing it at first.

"So, what if I did some things I'm not proud of? You will no longer be my friend. Is that it?"

It depends on what you did, or what you're still doing. No, I didn't say that. I was playing dumb for the whole remaining time. It was the early sunset when we said goodbye to his parents and villagers. We were in the car on our way back to the city. We both hesitated to break the awkward silence.

"OK." There was a dramatic pause that preceded the unpleasant revelations. "I haven't hurt a living soul in my life. I have never done anything illegal. I just never missed an opportunity to make more money." Another pause, but this a bit longer. "So, what's wrong in owning a few striptease bars here and there? It's all legit. You should know me by now. I'm a good person and more than a fair employer."

"Why do you need that? You're doing just fine. I don't understand. Why? You're the sharpest self-made entrepreneur I've ever met in my life. Why?"

"Sorry, but you can't understand. You need to diversify to survive. It has always been like this. Can't you see? Don't you agree?"

What an interesting choice of words for someone with only elementary formal education. No disrespect and no prejudice. Diversify. Wow!

I asked Baby to stop the car. I needed to get out ASAP. I wasn't angry. I wasn't disappointed. I didn't slam the door behind me.

"Hey, what about my book?"

"Check your email next week. It will be all there. Don't worry about that."

"I will reward you, buddy. You're my friend. This means a lot to me. You mean a lot to me."

"No disrespect, Baby, but the money you planned for me, I would like to be donated to your village. You know, that small black notebook."

I have never seen or heard from Baby since that night. I delivered the book about his incredible business journey as promised in the last letter. Honestly speaking, he spent more money on the food and drinks "marking" each chapter in his style than what I was supposed to get at the end. So, no harm is done. We are cool. I haven't changed my mind to this day. I just know and feel that Baby honored our agreement and my wish.

The irony was that a book about him missed a few dark pages or chapters of his business history. But, that's not my problem. Baby will have to live with that, not me. One question remains unanswered, though.

Al Pacino had his devil's advocate. Did Baby have his devil's ghostwriter?

I'm absolutely certain about one thing: "I'm (no longer) a fan of (that) man!"

Baby goodbye!

*The Silicon Valley Dogs
That Bark At Your
Startup First
Will Also Be The First
To Wag A Tail
When You Succeed*

MY NEIGHBOR - STEVEN JOBSKY

L ocation is everything. You know what I'm talking about, don't you? Entrepreneurs and founders, not startups and companies.

As far as I'm concerned, you can register, build, or do whatever you like with your company - on the North Pole. What difference does it make? Yes, it does, but you can still make it.

What? You have some heartbreaking slumdog millionaire story to share. Sorry, but I'm not interested. I'm not afraid, but I'm aware it's pointless to say anything about (who'd even dare to use "against" instead of "about") the sacred cows of the entrepreneurship universe. It's just the way things are and have always been.

I'm biased, but let me state something obvious.

If Nikola Tesla hadn't moved to the USA, he would've ended up being a priest like his father; also, a priest had always wanted for him. That's what I have on my mind when I write about locations in this story.

Do you have to be born at the right time and at the right place, and in the right family (optional, desirable, ideally)? Is all that it takes for someone eventually comes down to changing a location? Let's see.

It's always nice to see a new face in your neighborhood, isn't it? The more unusual your new neighbor is, the better.

So, a few years ago, an elderly man in his late sixties moved into one of our building's adapted (habitable) garages. The garages have cult status among entrepreneurs and founders. This isn't the case with my new neighbor. The stairs have been his nemesis for quite some time. The combination of poor genes and an even worse unhealthy lifestyle are to be blamed. I found his arrival in this fully transformed garage to be rather symbolic.

I was among the first to offer a helping hand in unloading a moving truck. Two groups of things caught my attention. First, there were a dozen computers of different models and sizes. Some of them could be considered ancient. Second, there were hundreds of books, mostly SF. Entire collections, some of them very rare.

Long repackaging story short, my new neighbor sacrificed a lot to keep his computers and books. In terms of furniture, clothes, and other things required for living, one word sums them all up perfectly - essentials.

Hear! Hear! Behold The Tech Pioneer!

What I feel is a mixture of guilt and ungratefulness. The story of my neighbor should be a long book, which I'm compressing into a short story.

First, we traveled into the distant future during our conversations about all the SF books we read. Then, we went back to the past as soon as computers became our main topic. His tech and entrepreneurship journey is a story worth writing and sharing.

There's nothing wrong with comparing my neighbor to Steve Jobs. I found it to be both useful and interesting. Here it goes. Judge for yourself.

My neighbor was born a few years later than Steve. Like Jobs, he spent his childhood and high school in the Eastern European version of California, the former Yugoslavia, during the 1960s and 1970s. Based not on Google and Wikipedia results, but my parents and my own first-hand experiences, I can say that a no-longer-existing country was an oasis of freedom, technological, and economic prosperity compared to the Eastern (Communist) Bloc. That's why I can't say that my neighbor was in a dramatically disadvantageous position compared to his US tech enthusiasts during that period.

They both developed a mindset of an engineer and became passionate about electronics thanks to their environment. Just to give you an example of how it used to work in the Socialist Federal Republic of Yugoslavia. As early as elementary school, the kids were given the freedom to choose which "newspaper" and magazines to read. That's how my neighbor got in love with technology and electronics. As a much younger countryman, I myself caught a few years of magazines about literature. Needless to say that all these interests were encouraged and sponsored by the state itself.

Both of them dropped out of college. Probably at the same time, a few years, give or take, both began their spiritual journeys of self-discovery and "spiritual enlightenment." The only difference is that Steven went to the far east, all the way to India. At the same time, my neighbor traveled to his cousins in Switzerland and Germany.

When they returned "enlightened," they entered into two different worlds. This is the moment where similarities died, and the difference became deep as an abyss.

Socialism vs. Capitalism - Public Ownership vs. Private Ownership

Steve was deep into entrepreneurship and fully independent waters, while my neighbor became a part of the controlled public companies. Socialism offered financial, healthcare security, and all kinds of benefits, but took away the choice of individual development and entrepreneurship.

For Jobs, computers were a matter of life and death. For my neighbor, a hobby and a personal, non-profit passion. Jobs was building his own computers, and my neighbor was assembling already existing computers. It wasn't an easy thing to do back then in the early 1980s in our former country. So, kudos to my neighbor. I had to Google just to get a glimpse of what he was talking about. I think that "his" first computer was Spectrum. How he was able to get all the parts is a story for itself.

There's a cheesy line, which wasn't far from the truth, that former Yugoslavia was neither West nor East. Some kind of a "hybrid." That's how my neighbor was able to work on the IBM systems in a socialist country.

If we can avoid the term "visionary," and settle for a problem-solver, I'd be grateful. Steve was making our world a better place with his Apple computers for profit. My neighbor wanted the same in his heavily bureaucratized publicly owned company. Meaning, he wanted to improve productivity as a part of his own private initiative. As a self-taught developer, he created an accounting program from scratch—one of the very first of its kind in the whole country. I had to Google because I've never even heard of Cobol. His reward wasn't the money or company's shares, not even a medal (you saw that in old communistic propaganda movies). Still, skepticism, indifference, and even envy among his colleagues and supervisors.

They both left their companies. It wasn't pleasant for either of them. While Jobs was busy with NeXT and Pixar, my neighbor created a completely new accounting program based on Access. Our country was collapsing. The civil war was on a destructive tour through former federal states until the full cycle of destruction was completed with the NATO bombing.

A few years after Jobs returned to Apple, my neighbor finally started his own company for accounting software solutions. The following years were the most productive for both entrepreneurs. Apple's iPod and iPhone models were taking the world by storm.

My neighbor's software did the same on an incomparably smaller scale on the remains of a once big and respectful market of former Yugoslavia. He didn't complain because he was finally free, independent, and creative as he'd always dreamed.

Sky's The Limit Until Life Revokes Its Permit

They were both struck down in the prime of their lives. Steve and my neighbor's wife were diagnosed with cancer.

I found a quote on Wikipedia from the 1995 documentary "Steve Jobs: The Last Interview." He was talking about computers.

"I feel fortunate to be at exactly the right place in Silicon Valley, at exactly the right time, historically, where this invention has taken form." This invention he was referring to was the computer.

On one occasion, I asked my neighbor, "Why didn't you leave our country? Why haven't you moved to the USA? Anywhere, but here."

"When I could have, I didn't want to. When I wanted to, I couldn't."

The story about Steve's adoption is one of the saddest I've ever read. Being huge SF fans, my neighbor and I discussed alternative realities among so many things we found in all those books. I wondered out loud, what would've happened, if my neighbor had been born in California instead of former Yugoslavia. He didn't like that idea at all, even if it was a theoretical one.

"I would have never met my wife, then. And, even if I did, there's no cure for cancer in California." We have never spoken about "what if" scenarios after that.

Yes, the locations are indeed everything, but without people, they're pointless and worthless—people we love and care about.

Yet, sometimes when I'm alone, I couldn't help myself to wonder - what if.

My neighbor would've never invented the iPod or iPhone. That has nothing to do with my point about the importance of location. He was and still is a problem-solver, after all. Had he been born somewhere near Silicon Valley, the accounting software wouldn't have been on his to-invent-and-to-do list, that's for sure. Maybe he would've done something completely different that had nothing to do with the computers and programming.

It takes more than one perfect element to give birth to a magic moment - in our history. Here's a nice quote. I just wrote and shared it with you for the first time.

Who am I to say to someone that they shouldn't admire Steve Jobs because of this or that? And, who are you to tell me that I couldn't admire my neighbor - Steven Jobsky? I'm using an iPhone. I hate accounting. I love SF. I finished this story. Time to call my neighbor. Time to travel to another galaxy. We are making plans for a spaceship that will use beer warp instead of warp drive. Wish us luck. Cheers!

Behind Every Successful Entrepreneur There Is A Wife With The Nerves of Steel

DESPERATE STARTUPWIVES

We keep reading and hearing about entrepreneurs. But, what about their wives?

Unless a superstar-entrepreneur's wife doesn't file for a divorce, we aren't very likely to find out more about her. Even then, we'd be more interested in how much she'd get as a part of a divorce settlement than how much she gave and contributed to her husband's success.

Well, this isn't one of those stories.

My Dear StartupWife - Gimme Five

My dear friend, the Engineer, was on his way to work. I can't recall what the reason his wife accompanied him that particular morning was. Let's just say that this lovely housewife had some business of her own to take care of.

They were using public transportation because my top-class friend couldn't afford a car. You know how it goes. Not much to talk about early in the morning. Especially if you were headed to a company that didn't appreciate your achievements.

"Look at it, baby. That's my building. I feel so proud." He was proud as a peacock. "Look. Over there. One of the tallest buildings in this part of Europe." I can confirm that he wasn't far away from the truth; give it or take a few floors.

The Engineer's wife wasn't thrilled about it at all. "First, that's not your building. You worked on it; you don't own it. That's a huge difference." She wasn't done. "Second, nothing to be proud of. Do you know how many nights I had to stay awake waiting for you to get home safe? So many things could've gone wrong."

"But, it didn't. I'm safe and sound, sitting next to my wife and looking at my masterpiece. You should be proud too. You could tell your sisters what I accomplished." The Engineer touched his glasses as if he wanted to emphasize his last line.

"I'd rather pass. Big building. Small reward. You promised we'd move to a bigger apartment. You also promised a car. It doesn't have to be new. Just saying. Haven't you deserved more? From one building to another. From one of your boss' promises to another. I'm sick and tired of all of these 'next time' empty promises."

Touché. The Engineer looked the other way. Suddenly, his "masterpiece" didn't look so impressive. He used to literally sleep on the construction site. It wasn't his building, but sure thing his heart was there - cemented. Almost literally. He didn't even notice when his wife got off the bus. She didn't plan to kiss him or even say, "see you tonight at home." Yup, he could call it even.

The Next Time - It'll All Be Fine

"Can you give us a hand?"

"Why do you have to ask?" The Engineer saw a lot of young smiley faces. He loved his team. The construction workers, who were preparing the tools, weren't as cold as buildings.

"Technically, you are our boss, boss." They laughed honestly and loudly with no intention to make the Engineer feel bad.

"Technically, you should've been packed and ready to go already. The new building won't build itself." He was helping and smiling at the same time. "You'll never change. I'll always have to keep an eye on you. Bunch of kids."

The "kids" became deadly serious and silent all of a sudden. Someone whispered, "the real boss is coming." The Engineer could hear the engine of a powerful machine roaring. He turned around. The brand new SUV, big as a house, headed straight toward them. The brakes had to scream to stop the four-wheel beast right on time before hitting anyone. The big bald guy came out of the car that was still running.

"What do you say, boys? She's a beauty, isn't she?" The owner was looking for approval and admiration.

"What happened to your Mercedes, boss?" Someone dared to ask.

"I let my wife have it. That's not a car for me, you know. I'm too big to drive it. Big boys need big toys." His smile asked for a human sacrifice. The workers laughed and nodded, but not the same way they did a few minutes ago when the Engineer arrived. "Don't you have to be somewhere, huh? C'mon, beat it!"

The workers were gone in a blink of an eye. The Engineer was alone with his boss at the company's lot.

"You're going to join them later. Right?" The boss looked surprised. "Everything OK?"

The Engineer hesitated. He couldn't tell if he was more ashamed or furious. He knew all too well what was about to happen. "Yes, but actually, I wanted to talk about... No, to ask you..."

"I know. I know. You don't have to say a thing. I feel you, my friend." The boss put his big arm around the Engineer. "I just need a couple more weeks, days, days. I'm caught between two projects. I didn't get all the money for the last building we finished, and I have to finance the new one. You know how it goes." If this was a silent movie, you'd think that a man in agony was struggling to catch a breath. "I owe you so much. I love you so much. I need you so much. You're my champion, and make no mistake about it. Your reward is on its way. You deserve so much more. God knows you do." With his other arm, the boss pressed his chests as if he was trying to keep the heart inside his chest.

The Engineer had a blurred vision of a giant anaconda wrapping around his neck. He needed to break free. He needed to speak out right here and right now. He was taking a deep breath. His eyes were blinking rapidly and uncontrollably.

"Is that my phone ringing? I must have left in the car." The big boss moved away with a surprising speed and ease, considering his size. "It stopped ringing, but I have to check. It may be important. It always is." He was scratching his head like a mad scientist on the brink of revolutionary discovery. "I'll get back to you. The next time we meet, it'll all be fine."

He jumped into the car and made a super-fast U-turn that would impress any cop in hot pursuit. The Engineer first rubbed his neck, and then he called his team leader.

"Can you please drive back to pick me up? No, it's OK. Get our boys what they want for breakfast. No, I'm good. You know my wife always makes me something. Yeah, she's taking care of my blood pressure and cholesterol. No, take your time. I will wait."

He opened his worn-out backpack. Two sandwiches as usual. No note. That's not usual for his wife. He got the message.

Either You'll Make Your Move,
OR I'm Moving Out

"Hey, baby. What are you doing here?"

The Engineer's wife was sitting on a washing machine soaking wet. The laundry was scattered all over the small bathroom.

"Our washing machine is dead. This time for good, and so am I, dead tired. I'm off to bed. Please let me through."

The Engineer was standing in the bathroom door speechless and motionless.

"What? What? What do you want? Do you need to hear my technical report?" She got into his face gritting her teeth.

"Why haven't you called someone to take care of it?"

She pushed him away and shouted in his ear on her way out of the bathroom. "Because we need a new washing machine. There's no "next time" for it. Capeesh?" The Engineer was reluctant for a moment. Should he pick up the half-washed clothes or go after his wife into the bedroom? "It can wait. She can't."

His wife was sitting on their bed. Her eyes were half-closed. Like being in a trance, she was singing something to herself slowly and silently.

"You can't be serious. 'Road to Nowhere.' Talking Heads. Do you want to drive me crazy? Is this your plan? What? I don't get it. Who are you?"

"No, I'm crazy because I watch my super-smart husband who's watering someone else's garden. No, I'm not crazy. You are the best example of an insane person. You know, the same thing over and over again. But, spoiler alert, no different results for you, baby."

"What would you have me do? To quit and move to another company. Is that it? Would that make you happy?"

The Engineer was demolished like a casino in Las Vegas with surgical precision. He was sitting on their bedroom's floor with his legs crossed. As if he was about to start meditating, but instead, on his knees, his hands were covering his face.

"No. That would mean the same problem with a different wrapper for us. I want you to start working for yourself. Be your own boss for a change."

She was calm, strong, and shart. The Engineer had never seen his wife like this. He was stunned.

"Either you'll make your move, or I'm moving out. Now, turn off the light. Close the door behind you. I'm tired. I need to sleep.

Night."

The Engineer was "Hypnotize" The Notorious B.I.G. TIME. Like a robot, he completed all of his wife's tasks and prepared himself for a long sleepless night. He was determined to welcome the morning with clean laundry and clean thoughts.

Epilogue

There are no secrets, and there's no shame among true friends. Our wives were on the same page about the perfect present we were to take with us to their new home. A new house needs a new washing machine. My friend Engineer and I were happy to invite two of our most reliable friends Jack (Daniels) and Johnnie (Walker). We agreed to sacrifice one of them right away, and keep the second bottle to welcome the little engineer who was still in his mom's stomach.

"I am an independent construction consultant now. Can you believe it?"

I nodded and raised my glass, asking for a toast.

"Don't be so modest, my darling. You're running your own company now. You have your team. You're choosing projects to work on." The Engineer's wife sneaked behind his back to hug and kiss him.

I couldn't miss an opportunity to tease him, even a little bit. "Whose idea was that? Just being curious and drunk." I hide my smile behind a glass.

"My husband has always had it in him. He just needed to be motivated the right way at the right time."

"I couldn't agree about the first part. As far as motivation is concerned, I'd not go down that rabbit hole." Time to change the tune. "At least we know who takes all the credits for this beautiful garden of yours." I nodded at the Engineer's wife.

"That's all me, actually." The Engineer surprised both my wife and me.

"He needs to be reminded every morning how important it is to water your own garden." The Engineer's wife spiced up her explanation with a smile. "Now, let's get inside. Our bellies need proper motivation. Mine twice as much."

We all followed her almost immediately.

"I'm afraid you're next, buddy." The Engineer whispered to my ear on the way into the house. "I'm pretty much sure, you'll have an interesting conversation with your wife on your way back."

"What do you mean? I don't get you."

"My wife can be very persuasive when it comes to 'gardening.' She's planting the entrepreneurship seeds in your wife's head as speak. Good luck, buddy."

The lunch was delicious, and my wife's facial expression was curious. Bon Appétit!

An Entrepreneur Who Wants To Go From Nothing To Everything Has To Risk, Give, or Lose Something

CRAZY, STUPID, YOUNG ENTREPRENEUR'S LOVE

What motivates entrepreneurs the most? Allow me to throw a rhyme here: Is it because of the money, fame, or because no two days are the same?

You know, it's easy to admire uber-successful-and-famous entrepreneurs. What were they as kids or even better as teenagers?

You see before-and-after pictures, and you think you know all there's to know about someone. You read a couple of heartwarming rags to riches stories, and you believe you've figured it all out.

I've always wanted to see entrepreneur cubs before their transformation into money-making machines. It's easier said than done for obvious reasons. Nobody walks around with a neon sign on their forehead: "one day I'm going to be a successful entrepreneur" or "pay attention, this is the future…"

It just doesn't work like this, or does it?

Daddy, Put Down The Gun, I'm Not Going To Marry This Young Man

"He's my simpatico," says my teenage daughter.

"I read that it's very important for parents to fully support the emotional development of their children at this age," elaborates my wife.

"I'm here for your pizza, but I agree with whatever you're talking about now," says our French poodle Fifi with her eyes.

I was surrounded and trapped at my most vulnerable moment. Nowadays, one can't have some privacy with his favorite pizza. Here it goes. They want something.

"He's so cute." You don't say.

"He's not her boyfriend, technically. They just have innocent childlike feelings for each other. That's all." You don't say.

"Hey fatty, where's my cut of your pizza?" The furry mobster racketeering me, as usual.

My pizza will get cold. I will boil. I'm all ears. Let's see what my ladies are up to this time.
"Mom wanted to ask you something. If it's OK with you, of course." My little girl is blushing like ketchup that will soon become cold lava. How appropriate, isn't it? The name of my favorite pizza was "Volcano Special."

"How about you take us all on the "Mountain" this Sunday?" The so-called "Mountain" is more of an impressive hill and a favorite picnic spot, but not even close to the real mountain. She also emphasized "us" and "all," which meant only one thing. Simpatico is coming too. "What do you say? Wouldn't that be great? We can walk a bit, have lunch, and get to know this boy better."

"I'm taking a shovel with me. I may need it, if I don't like him." The last time my daughter's eyes were that big was when she saw Fifi for the first time. My wife poked her elbow in my ribs. "Daddy is joking, little one." She smiled.

"If we really like him, I may just throw him out of the car while I'm still driving." I quickly raised my hands in surrender. One more blow in my ribs, and I'd have to change my favorite sleeping position tonight. "I'm joking. What happened to your sense of humor?"

"It's our daughter's first simpatico. This is important."

"OK. You got yourself a deal. It's official." My daughter hugged me around my neck and kissed my cheeks. Two seconds later, she was gone.

"I'm so proud of you. We're doing the right thing. I thought you'll be more stubborn. Good thing you weren't." She was scratching her elbows on her way out of the kitchen.

"They got what they wanted. Now, you and I are going to finish this pizza in peace." I couldn't only see a wagging tail. "You girls stick together. How typical." Little did they know that I still had one card left up to my sleeve.

A Young Man, Who Talks The Talk, and Walks The Walk, For Real

"Hey, why don't you come with me? Five miles. Do you think you can make it?" Of course, he took my bait. I got my mano-a-mano time.

My daughter looked disappointed, and I was sure she wanted to complain. But my lady backed me up on this one. "Let's make some sandwiches. Our boys will be hungry when they get back. Don't be like that. You have to learn to compromise. The sooner, the better."

On my way down the hill with a young boy, I could see my wife's thumb up. I sure hope my little girl didn't use any sign language to express her feelings at that moment.

"So, here we are." What should I ask first? Ah, the usual. "How's school?"

"I dropped out of school, Sir." He looked me in the eye without blinking. A straight answer with not even remote traits of shame.

"Why? If I'm right, you're sixteen." I didn't want to sound judgy. But we planned for five miles. This was my first question.

"I have to work, Sir." He was honest and direct to the bone. I had to give him that.

"Please don't "Sir" me. We are way past formalities. Why do you have to work?" When I look back at that day, maybe I should've been more thoughtful and more polite when shooting all those questions at him. But hey, it's my kid we're talking about.

"My father left us when I was still a baby. My younger sister is still in elementary school. My older sister is studying. She works as a waitress only on weekends. My mother's salary can't barely cover our rent and bills. My mother used to work two jobs at once. I needed to do something about that. I'm the man of the house. It's my responsibility."

I lost breath, but walking uphill had nothing to do with it. "Let's sit here on a bench and rest for a while, please." Somebody just unloaded a ton of bricks on my chest. "What do you do? Where do you work?"

"I'm a construction worker." He saw that look in my eyes, so he rushed it to continue. "I started with just ten euros per day. In less than a year, I proved myself to be a quick learner and hard worker. Now, I get fifty euros per day plus two meals. I don't work on Sundays, this is why I could come with you today. My boss treats me fairly. I get paid for overtime work, and I also get bonuses when I stay as long as it's needed to finish the work."

He didn't want me to feel sorry for him. I was more than sure about it.

"Can I ask you something, Sir? I mean no, Sir, you said that's OK."

"Feel free to do both; use my first name and ask."

"I'm curious. Where were you at my age? Your daughter says that you write for a living. You must have spent a lot of time studying. Right?"

"I used to wear a uniform when I was your age. I left home to become a military cadet."

"What happened, if you don't mind me asking? Aren't you supposed to be a colonel or something?"

"Well, not exactly. I got expelled from the military academy. I got a law degree five years later." He looked at me speechless with his mouth wide open. I knew he was too embarrassed to ask. "I was dishonorably discharged because of a girl. I wanted to spend more time with her, but instead, I ended up in a military prison. More than once, for the record."

"Wow! That's just awesome! Your wife must be proud. You did all those things for her. It's like in the movies." Ah, Millennials. I hoped he didn't have too much time to watch movies. He was way too young for "An Officer and a Gentleman" starring Richard Gere.

"Hm, that girl didn't become my wife. She'd married someone else. I'd appreciate it if you don't mention this part of our conversation over lunch." He nodded more than I could count. "Life isn't a movie, but you know that already all too well. Let's get back. We will live to fight some other day. Better to say, we will eat to walk some other day."

He liked both my joke and the idea. I felt terrible. For Pete's sake, this was supposed to be his day off. My girls were surprised and worried to see us again so early, especially the little one. I hugged him and told another joke just for my girls to see him laughing. During lunch, I treated him as one of my army buddies. He absolutely deserved it.

We stayed until the evening. We, the parents, granted the young wannabe couple permission to walk around with Fifi.

"So, what do you think about him?" My wife couldn't wait to ask.

"Ecce Homo!" I had a tear in my eye when I said that.

It's Fair To Compare - Behold The Rich Heir

The next weekend, we had old friends over for dinner. A couple with a single child, just like us.

Their son and our daughter have known each other since kindergarten. They went to the same class in elementary school. Now, they're attending different high schools. However, that's not stopping them from spending a lot of time together. They have been besties for as long as my wife and I can remember.

Either our daughter was at their house, or bestie was with us. It was like that almost every single day. They also have the same friends. His parents didn't have so much free time. We did our best to catch up during the weekends.

The kids were playing video games in my daughter's room. Our wives were discussing the latest breakthroughs when it comes to diets over a dining table. We, the fathers and husbands, grabbed the opportunity to claim our apartment's terrace—the best place to enjoy cigars and private conversations.

I told him about my daughter's simpatico I met the previous weekend. I could tell that the story touched him deeply.

"Oh man, that boy's story brings back old memories. You know what I'm talking about, don't you?"

"Sure, I do." My friend had to fight tooth and nail to get an exclusive distribution agreement for one well-known sportswear brand. He also dropped out of high school. He made his first money as a reseller of anything he could get his hand on, mostly fruits and vegetables. Countless nights spent in a small van waiting for outdoor markets to open. Driving from one place to another, searching for the best deals and prices.

I had nothing but the utmost respect for that hard-working and determined man. Eventually, he got his reward with that exclusive distribution agreement, ensuring both respect and wealth for his family.

"I feel for that young man, but I shouldn't be worried about him if I were you. If he manages to stay on the right path, he's going to make something of himself. Guaranteed."

"I agree. He's already paying a high price for having to man up almost overnight." I light another cigarette.

"What do you mean? All the pain and troubles will pay off big time. He will learn some tough life and business lessons the hard way, but it's going to be worth it for him."

"I know. But I'm talking about all that time he could've enjoyed. He will never be young again."

My friend didn't like what I just said. He didn't bother to hide it. "At least he isn't wasting time on video games like my little prince and your princess. I don't even have to go to check on them. They haven't moved away from the screen since we arrived. I'm sure of it."

He was right. The kids refused to come and join us for dinner. Our wives had to order them a pizza. Thinking about the devils.

"Look at them, my dear. They've completely forgotten about us." My friend's wife was laughing while my wife made sure their wine glasses stayed full. Then she pointed her finger at me. "I've always thought that we are going to be in-laws. What's with this poor boy your wife is telling me all about?"

"You're crossing a line here, dear. Obviously, it's the wine that does all the talking. I apologize on my wife's behalf." My friend was angry and embarrassed. I'm sure that Superman's laser beam would suit my friend perfectly.

"In wine, there's truth. And the truth is, money talks, poor kid works."

"That does it. Enough. Thank you for a beautiful evening and a great dinner. We will show ourselves out. I will go to get our son."

It seemed that my friend's words made all the wine evaporate almost instantly. His wife put down a glass. She cast her eyes down on her way out.

A Girl Reckless And A Beautiful Necklace

I was home alone working on some articles. My girls were out shopping. Fifi was making my company. All of a sudden, she started barking. While I figured out what was going on, she was already all ears behind our apartment's front door. Someone is standing outside our door. The doorbell was silent. No knocking. Yet, I had to open the door and check. Fifi is so attached to our girls that every sound around the door gets her full attention.

"I apologize. I was about to ring a bell to check if you are home. I'm so sorry. I didn't mean to cause any trouble."

Simpatico was shaking. Fifi was running and jumping on his legs. I was surprised, but I didn't feel uncomfortable.

"Don't you just stand there. C'mon get it. You are more than welcome. No need to apologize." I moved aside to let him and Fifi in. I closed the door. He didn't dare to look me in the eye. He was holding something that looked like a nicely wrapped gift.

"I just want to leave something for your daughter, and I will be on my way right away."

"Forget about it. No way. It's your first time here in our home. Please." I showed him to follow me to the living room. He wanted to be here; otherwise, the postal service was still alive and kicking the last time I checked. "Please, sit down and relax. Would you like something to drink?"

"No, thank you, I'm good. I just wanted to leave this." He put his gift next to him. Fifi was nesting in his lap. She waited patiently to cuddle. The young boy was grateful that Fifi gave him an excuse to avoid direct eye contact with me.

"I'm so sorry you missed her. Should I give my daughter a call? They should hurry up to get back home. We have a guest waiting."

"No. No, please." He blushed. "I planned to leave this at your doorstep. I feel so uncomfortable."

"Really, no need for that. You'd be surprised, but I also used to be young once. You are a good kid." I avoided using the words "foolish" and "in love." But I had to know what was going on and why. "Is everything OK?"

"Well, this is my farewell present. I won't be seeing your daughter anymore."

"Why? What happened? I don't mean to pry, but I'd really like to know. If you don't mind, of course."

The young man's eyes were full of tears, but his voice was overwhelmingly strong and confident.

"Your daughter's friends don't accept me. They make fun of me. The way I dress, talk, and even behave. I see nothing wrong with me. I didn't say or did anything bad."

"Did my daughter take part in it?"
"No. No. But she said that she didn't want to choose between her friends and me. I should get along with them. How? They will never accept me. Right?" I looked down. We both knew the answer to that question. "One day, I will be someone worth respecting. I will be my own man. I will have my own construction company."

"They will always be kids even when they grow up. Their wealthy parents aren't going to live forever. What do you think will happen next? You will outmatch them in any way possible. The Force is strong with you." I tried to cheer him up. If Star Wars couldn't help, then I didn't know what else possibly would.

"I am not a Jedi, Sir. I like the Siths more. Do you know why?"

Oh dear, what did I do? I just made things worse with my stupid joke. Life isn't a joke for this young man. I should've known better.

"There's a line everybody missed. 'Only a Sith deals in absolutes.' That's me. That's who I want to be."

"What's that supposed to mean?" My eyes full of fear gave me away. He wouldn't do something foolish, would he? He read me good like a bad book.

"It means all or nothing. There's no middle ground. No compromise. I will prove them all wrong. They say that success is the best revenge. Whoever said that was absolutely right." I was speechless. "You don't have to worry about me, Sir. I won't do anything stupid. I'm poor, but I'm not mean. Please make sure your daughter gets my gift. Thank you and goodbye."

He was gone before I could pull myself together to say something. Fifi was sniffing the gift. I knew it was the wrong thing to do, but I had to open it. I needed to know what was in that small box-shaped gift.

It was a beautiful silver necklace. Even though it was made out of silver and not gold, I could tell it wasn't a cheap one. How many hours or days did this young man have to work for it? My rich friend, who was our guest with his wife and son a few nights ago, was right about this young boy. His life's story brings back old memories. I used to be just like him.

"C'mon Fifi! Let's go out for a walk. Let's just walk and don't talk."

*Some Startups Are Built To Last
Some Only To Sell Fast*

WHAT'S UP WHATSAPP 2.0?

Why are so many startups built now, only to sell later? Trust me, this question doesn't bother me one bit.

When you literally lose count of how many startups you've written the content for, you simply forget to care. That's not, and it has never been my problem. One thing I learned, though.

Startup founders who just want to make a quick buck are "rewarded" with slow regret, period. It has been proven a million times. Case closed.

It's a long list of startups I used to write for. Do you know how many of these startups survived the first couple of years? Do you know how many lived long enough to go public? Only one! The rest of them either failed or were sold.

I have no intention to bombard you with countless real-life examples. I just need two to make my point. Let's begin with the first one.

The Sign On The Gates of Startup Hell: I Just Can't Wait To Sell!

You just can't make this stuff up.

Believe it or not, there was a founder with a "brilliant" and "original" idea to create his own version (read: replica) of WhatsApp. I kid you not.

I thought, just the thing the world needs: another WhatsApp, but

I kept it to myself. Hey, it's your money, so knock yourself out. But, here's the thing about the startup founders. They're always high on enthusiasm, and they can't keep their mouth shut. So, I had to write and listen at the same time.

Please don't get me wrong. It's easy to be a wise guy. I really admire people who're actually trying to create something for a change. And, above all, who put their money where their mouth is. Not because they're paying for my writing, but because there's a bunch of fellow freelancers who get hired during the process (designers, developers, translators, etc.).

But, here's the thing. This guy and other startup founders, just like him, kept making the same mistakes and repeating the same line. "I'm going to sell it. I'm going to sell it."

They didn't even finish their websites or tested their apps, and they're already counting the money from the hypothetical takeovers. "Do you know how much money this or that founder got for selling his startup? Do you know? Do you know?" I'm listening to my client-wannabe-founder, and I can't believe how big their eyes become when they talk about these things. They fell in some kind of trance stone-cold sober and without any kind of substance in sight.

You're writing, and you can't believe how people waste their time and money so recklessly and easily. But hey, who am I to wake you from your startup built-only-to-sell-startup dreams? Right? So, I do my work. I take my money. I move on.

Thanks To The Different Perception - Here's An Exception

Thank God for this startup minority report.

These founders were different, and they did things differently from the very beginning.

I can't get too much into details. Here's what I can share. They created some software solution (technically an app), one uber-popular global brand can't imagine a single day without. They're using it for creating brochures and catalogs that are later printed and distributed. I'm talking about thousands of employees (users). The corporation is paying a monthly license for every single one of them. The corporation is also saving millions of dollars each year thanks to this solution. So, it's the fairest win-win scenario you could possibly imagine.

This time I was the one who couldn't keep it to himself for a change. I just had to know and ask. We spent some time working together, so I could allow myself the luxury of being direct.

"So, why aren't you selling? I know your situation. You invested everything you have and even what you don't have into development and marketing. The banks are breathing down your necks. What are you waiting for?"

These guys, brothers, by the way, were and still are something. Do you remember that famous scene from the movie "Troy?" The small messenger boy says to Achilles (Brad Pit), "The Thessalonian you're fighting, he's the biggest man I've ever seen. I wouldn't want to fight him." Brad nailed him with this timeless line, "That is why no one will remember your name."

I was that messenger boy in this situation, and I was talking to Achilles, who had a twin brother.

"Hey, we didn't get into all of this to sell. Our startup lives and dies with us." The other brother took it from here. It felt like one person was delivering this powerful speech.

"This is something we're going to leave to our kids. Our startup isn't for sale. Not now, not ever."

I was Disney frozen. What are you supposed to say after hearing something like this? Nothing. You write a story about it.

"At one point, you invest yourself so much that it becomes impossible to sell. There's no money in the world to make you give away your startup baby." I wasn't sure which one of the brothers said that, but who cares. At that particular moment, I realized something important.

It's not the idea. It's the attitude that makes all the difference.

There's nothing wrong with being rightfully compensated for all of your startup troubles. You fight, bleed, grow, so one day, you can drink a beer and enjoy the sunsets on your private island for the rest of your days. Or whatever makes you and your loved ones happy.

And, yes, there are startup magicians, who build to sell. And then, they build something else again, and they sell it again. More than once. Each time successfully. That's a legit thing to do, also worth respecting.

To Sell or Not To Sell - That's Your Startup's Question Now

Time to wrap up my story. If you've just started to build something and you're already thinking about selling it - good luck with that. Unfortunately, greed and impatience are the biggest mass startup killers in business history.

I have to go. The next startup is waiting for the content to be written. Let's see what these guys are made of. Are they already dreaming about selling, or are they determined to keep fighting and keeping their startup for themselves?

*A Lucky Entrepreneur Is Both
A Founder and CEO
A Successful One Is
Still Founder
But Has Someone Else
As His Startup's CEO*

THE ENTREPRENEUR WHO WOULD BE KING

They say that the devil is in the details. I disagree. I say, the entrepreneurship devil is hiding in plain sight.

Take LinkedIn for an example. There are three phases both a startup and its founder have to go through together.

First, you see a company. The person who created it is simply - the founder. The company is still in startup diapers.

Then, this person, an entrepreneur, adds a CEO title. So, he's no longer only a founder, but both a founder and a CEO. We're talking about a serious company now. It's no longer a question of whether or not this company, a former startup, will survive, but how big it will become.

Finally, you see the same company, but something has changed. The founder is the same person, but someone else is now a CEO. You are no longer dealing with a company, but with a business empire.

What happens when a founder can't detach himself from a CEO title and role?

My PRECIOUS!! We Wants It! We Needs It!

I used to be in a position to follow one startup through all three metamorphosis phases. I'd come and go as work requested. First, I wrote for a startup. Then, I created content for a fast-growing company. Finally, my words became a part of the business kingdom.

Of all the people, I have met since this startup was launched, I recognized only two: the founder and his right-hand man. In the GoT terms, the King and the Hand of the King (the Hand).

"He should be playing golf, fishing, or whatever makes him happy. I don't get it. Look at him. Is that him supervising the lawnmower men as we speak, in person?"

I was sitting in the Hand's office. We were drinking coffee and looking at what was going on in front of the company's building. We have known each other for years. We have been through thick and thin from this startup's day one. That's why I could dare to talk like that behind the King's back. I trusted the Hand with my life. Strange as it may look to you, we both loved and respected the King.

"I hear you, my old friend. But that's the King. He's never going to change." The Hand has been working for the King for almost ten years now. The King hired him right after college. This company's number two has always been loyal and painfully true.

"Have you tried to talk to him? You have grown. Things aren't that simple as they used to be. Quite a few people to keep an eye on. It's about time for him to stop being both founder and CEO."

The Hand was scratching his head nervously. It's not that I hit his nerve, but I could see that he was tired of the same old story.

"I just gave up. He thinks that no one is good enough to be his company's CEO. He feels threatened, which is ridiculous. He wouldn't retire. He would have more time to rest and intervene only when he really has to."

"Not even you?"

Perhaps I cut deeper than I should this time. The Hand took a deep breath.

"The King doesn't even consider promoting his own sons into CEOs. What are you talking about? You can be serious. I've been well taken care of. You know that."

"But you aren't rewarded. I also know that you bled for this company. You're the heart and soul of it. The King can still keep up. One day he's going to start losing it. Don't you think it'd be too late to do something about it?"

"It's already too late. We've already crossed that line. I didn't tell you. We have already filed for an IPO. I will get my package of shares. That's it."

We both went silent. Each one occupied with his own thoughts, hopes, and worries.

"Don't you two schmucks have some work to do? What am I paying for?" We didn't notice that the King was back. He was walking toward us, laughing loudly. Arms wide open for a bone-crushing hug. The King at his both finest and typical business modus. "Where have you been, you writing weasel? You come and go as you want."

"As I'm needed, Sir. A wise man once told me that freedom is priceless."
"Who was that wise man? Who told you that?"

"It was you, Sir."

"Ah, you silver-tongued devil." He grabbed my head with his big hands as gently as he could. "How about lunch? I have some new blog topics to discuss with you."

"I thought you have a person who's in charge of marketing and content."

"Yes, we do, but this is a special assignment. You have always been my special ops guy. Up we go!" On our way out of the Hand's office, the King just waved at him with not a single word said.

The Blessing of the Corporate Flying Dutchman

I was flattered that a company's alpha and omega could find time to talk about blog topics. Talking about the time, I couldn't help myself not to poke a bear.

"How do you find time to be in so many places and meet with so many people, almost every single day, Sir?"

"There's no room for "almost" in my dictionary. It has been like this every single day for the last ten years. There's no rest for the wicked, although I don't like that word - wicked. I'm not wicked. I'm just tireless."

I didn't doubt that. I just wondered if the King was fully aware of what was going on in his company? They say that our civilization has evolved and developed beyond all expectations. Perhaps too quickly. They also say that our body, especially the brain, has a serious problem catching up with progress. As far as nature is concerned, our brain and basic instincts are still stuck in the stone age. The King still thinks and acts as if his startup is in the first phase. The truth is that he's running a big company that's about to go public.

"Imagine what you could achieve with a few CEOs and COOs." I didn't want to sound disrespectful, so I added. "Just thinking out loud, if you don't mind, Sir."

"Let me tell you something about business, the way I see and run it. You must have seen 'Pirates of the Caribbean.' Right?"

"More than once, Sir. That's my daughter's favorite franchise."
"My grandchildren are crazy about those movies too. They love that clown, Captain Jack Sparrow. Kids. What do they know?" The King filled up our glasses with the grimace of disapproval. "But do you know who the real hero is?"

Who would say that the King was an expert when it comes to this franchise. He must have spent a lot of time watching all the sequels with his grandchildren. My face turned into one huge question mark. I really wanted to know.

"Captain Davy Jones!"

"Who? You can't be serious." I had to soften my tone. "What do you mean, Sir?"

"He gave his heart and soul to his ship, didn't he?" I nodded. I wanted to throw in a couple of details about the captain's "unselfish and spontaneous sacrifice,' but the King was quicker. "My company is my ship. Without the captain, there is no ship. There is nothing."

Yup, you're the captain of your ship, alright. Your 'crew,' your employees are thrilled, just like in the movie.

"If someone wants to take my place, then the ultimate sacrifice has to be made. You can't run my company without giving yourself up completely to it."

OK. The Hand was right. Now, I know why the company won't have a CEO as long as the King is alive.

"How about the second in command? Every great leader had his most trusted and skillful general." Let's go to the stars. "For example, in 'Star Trek, ' Jean-Luc Picard could always rely on his 'Number One.' And he was still the captain of the spaceship. Nobody questioned his authority."

"I don't watch that space rubbish. I don't know what you're talking about."

You mean, your kids aren't the 'Star Trek' fans. I just had enough of movies, and TV shows comparisons and metaphors.

"My apologies, Sir. It's your company."

"Yes, it is. You're damn right it is. I built it from scratch with nothing but my bare hands. I could destroy it if I want to. It's my right. I can do whatever I want with it."

The King is alive! Long live the King!

I don't know what happened to the King's company, and honestly, I don't care. Succession is a tricky thing for both big companies and empires. Did his sons take over, eventually? Did the Hand convince his King that he would be a proper 'replacement?'

They say that the captain goes down with the ship. The founders don't have to go down with their startups. But what do I know? Would I share a co-authorship over my book with my wife? I don't think so. I don't judge because I don't like to be judged.

*The Size Doesn't Matter
In Entrepreneurship
As Long As You're
The Captain of Your Own Ship*

BLUE COLLAR ENTREPRENEURS BLUES

My wife always wanted to do something with our old closets. So, we finally found and invited two professional carpenters with the most impressive portfolio in this field.

You know how it goes, don't you? She was in charge of instructions and creative advice. On the other hand, I was in charge of the beer. And, you know that where is beer there are inevitable questions—one of the most annoying ones.

What do you do for a living?

Oh dear, here we go again. I was thinking about what I was supposed to say. I was considering a couple of the most likely probable scenarios.

I'm a freelance writer. Where are your books? I write for websites. We have or don't have a website. Would you mind having a look? Maybe, you can write something for us. Is that a great idea? Cheers!

You see, I was already underestimating and judging the guys without saying a 'hello.'

It's just like one of the guys was reading my mind, or maybe I lost track of time. It had become pretty much obvious that I was worried about the best possible answer to a question that hadn't even been asked.

"You don't have to worry, buddy." One of the carpenters spoke up. "When we entered your home, we saw that your laptop was turned on. It's the middle of the working week, so you probably work from home."

His colleague and co-owner of their company jumped in. "Judging by your handshake, you have soft hands. It's like you're playing the piano or something." They both laughed.

"Either way, you have been probably expecting us to ask a polite question to start a conversation while we work. That's OK. We don't mind. It has been that obvious."

They got me cornered, fair, and square. They were really good at finishing each other's sentences. It seemed that it wasn't enough to be good with wood and screws in their line of work. You had to be good at reading people too—especially the ones who were supposed to pay for your work.

Money For Nothin' and Business Advice For Free

They were working and talking at the same time. These guys were not one but two steps ahead of me.

"Yes, you guessed right. We have a website. But here's the thing. We invested a lot of money, so it looks professional. We also invested money in Google ads. This is how you found us in the first place." Wow! These guys did their business homework properly.

"So, you can be totally relaxed. We don't need your help, nor do we plan to bother you with questions about the Internet and stuff." They even knew when the right time for a dramatic pause was before making their final point. "We may be carpenters, but we consider ourselves to be 21st-century carpenters."

"Cyber-carpenters." The other added, laughing.

Wow, number two! Touché!

Needless to say, I was totally stunned and speechless. This wasn't something I expected. There was no way I could have seen this one coming.

So, I did the only thing I could possibly do in this situation. I offered more beer, and I asked if there was something more I could do to make their job more pleasant and easier. The carpenters with the amazing Sherlock Holmes deductive skills had an interesting idea.

"Why don't you look for 'Money For Nothing' on YouTube and play it while we work. Do you know that song?"

"Dire Straits. Everybody knows that song. It's a classic." Rock 'n' roll cyber-carpenters. What a time to be alive.

"But, do you know what this song is really about?" The question caught me in the middle of the YouTube search on my phone.

One of the best guitar riffs of all time lightened up the mood. "I'm all ears. Enlighten me, my dear friend. I'm all ears." There was no sarcasm in my voice. It sounded more like a challenge. The carpenter smiled. Challenge accepted, as it seemed.

"Well, the story goes that the guy who wrote the song had some guys working something for him in his kitchen." The carpenters laughed. "Or, he saw some guys working and couldn't help himself from overhearing their conversation. Something like, I can't remember exactly. Either way, there was some popular song on TV. When you hear the 'Money For Nothing,' you get it right away that these workers didn't think highly of the musicians."

"I see. It makes sense. Is there more to it?"

"This is how the phrase 'money for nothing' was used to describe their music work. We are biased." The other carpenter nodded and shrugged his shoulders as if he was apologizing. "These workers thought that what they were doing was real work for real money. We don't think so. We respect every man's work, and so should you too."

"I have never said anything about your work. I haven't been disrespectful."

"True. But your silence was deafening when we arrived. Sometimes, even thoughts can be disrespectful. Agree?"

"Huh. OK. I will give you that. So, now what?"

"Now, you're going to play us that song again. And, while you're at it, bring us two more beers."

So, what happened next?

These guys did an amazing renovation job. I had to admit that the good old 'Dire Straits' song sounded a little bit different. And, yes, my attitude went through a thorough renovation process too.

Don't judge books by their covers. And, don't judge entrepreneurs, especially carpenters, by their numbers.

"You know, I'm happy with our closets' new look. What do you think about our kitchen?" My wife was already going through ads on her phone. "We should find a good plumber."

I had a clear vision of a plumber in a spacesuit who's landing in front of our door on a drone. "It can wait." I left my wife puzzled and went to my room as quickly as I could.

The Four Horsemen of The Startupocalypse
HIGH
- Half-Heartedness
- Impatience
- Greed
- Hesitance

A TALE OF TWO CO-FOUNDERS

Two best friends since childhood. They were like brothers, but without 'like.' One entrepreneurship heart and mind, two bodies.

They launched a startup. They worked on one of those apps, we nowadays take for granted, around the clock. Sometimes I felt that I should be the one paying them for the privilege of being in their company. I got paid for my writings and rewarded with unlimited positive vibes.

The world was their to take. Life was good. The initial team was growing.

What was that saying for a company and a crowd? Ah, two is a company, three is a crowd. Right? No, it's not what you're thinking right now. It wasn't a girl or the third business partner who ruined this startup fairy tale.

The third element that was nowhere to be found when they were just starting out, suddenly became so abundant, they didn't know what to do with it. Yes, I'm talking about money. The number of app users was growing exponentially. Their idea was raining money.

It seemed that nothing could stand in their way of well-deserved success.

Temptations of the Dance Floor

"Have I ever told you that I have a law degree?"

"What?" Both co-founders had puzzled looks on their faces. "What do you mean? You're our writer. We didn't know you're a lawyer too. Wow! Kudos!"

"I'm not a lawyer. I haven't passed a bar exam. I did some work as a freelance paralegal, and that's it. Mostly simple contracts, Terms of Service, and Privacy Policies for websites and apps."

"OK. We still don't get you. Both our website and app are covered with all terms and policies stuff we could possibly need." They looked at each other in wonder. "If you wanted to take care of it, why didn't you say so? You could've taken the money."

"Guys. Guys, you're getting me all wrong here. I'm not talking about your website or the app."

Finally, I got their full attention. They were looking at me without blinking. I owed them an explanation. OK. Here we go.

"I'm talking about you guys. To be more precise, about a contract between you two."

They kept a serious look on their faces, and then they burst into uncontrollable laughter.

"Oh man, you're so good. You almost got us. Don't do that man, that's dangerous." The other co-founder agreed. "Yup, my heart almost stopped. You got me worried that we've missed something. You're crazy. That's why we love you."

I was looking at two co-founders who behaved like kids. They were laughing and simulating a friendly boxing match as if I wasn't there.

"Guys! Guys! Can you get serious for a moment, please? It's for your own good. I think that you really need a contract."

"Why would we need a contract for? We're cool. We're brothers. Who needs a stupid piece of paper? Right, my brother?" The other co-founder nodded and quickly threw a sucker punch.

"Are you insane? What's wrong with you? This hurts, man."

"I'm so sorry. I didn't mean that. We're kidding, man. Are you OK? Let me have a look?" The co-founder who pretended to be hurt grabbed his business partner and a friend. Now, they were on the floor wrestling.

"Guys, can I say what I have to say? Just two minutes, and I will be on my way. Please."

"You have one minute." They just couldn't stop laughing and wrestling. I had the word 'seriously' written all over my face. They were up and serious for a change. "One minute. Shoot."

"You should have something on a paper to regulate your professional relationship, just in case."

"What case? What are you talking about?" They looked at me as if I just killed one of them. "No negative vibes, man. We hired you because you are a great guy. What has gotten into you? This isn't you."

"What could possibly go wrong? Would you turn on me, my brother?" One head. Two different voices. That was how I felt.

"Never, my brother. There's no money in the world. No way." Then they turned on me.

"Hey you, black raven. Chill out and get back with some good vibes."

"Yeah, what was that all about? Are you having some bad trip or what?"

I decided that my words had been falling on deaf ears long enough. "My bad, guys. You know the song. 'My intentions were good; please don't let me be misunderstood.' Apologies. See you tomorrow. OK?"

"That's much better. You're right. We need some music to cheer up."

"We are cool. We love you, man. You know that. Come over here."

I hugged both of them. I also apologized one more time. I was good to go. My conscience was clear. On my way out of their office, I had one more look at them. Ignorance is bliss, isn't it?

The First Co-Founder

"Thank you for agreeing to see me. I really appreciate it."

"Where is…"

"He won't be joining us tonight. It's just you and me. I wanted to consult with you about something. I hope that's OK with you?"

This wasn't the first time for me to meet with one of the co-founders after working hours. We had this great friendly relationship. So, nothing out of the ordinary. Except for the fact that we weren't even near their office. It was a bit late. Finally, it was one of those places where people value more privacy than what's on the menu. The whole situation I found myself in had this not-so-subtle tone of conspiracy.

"Yeah, it's OK. I'm always here for you." I quickly added. "For both of you." I was determined to get straight to the point. The sooner, the better. "So, what's up?"

"I've been thinking." He hit the pause button. He wanted to make sure I was paying full attention to what he was to say next. "It was my idea for the app, you know. This is how the whole thing started."

That was an interesting choice of words - "whole" instead of "our." Something was definitely going on between the two co-founders. It had been a couple of weeks since our conversation about the contract. I just wanted to make sure I wasn't Leonardo DiCaprio in this version of 'Inception.'

"This, whatever it is, has nothing to do with me just mentioning the idea of a contract. Right? I need to know that. We need to be clear about it. OK?"

"I should've listened to you more carefully that day. We aren't the first startup you've been working with? You have seen these situations before, haven't you?" He was looking at me as if I was holding a crystal ball in my hands.

"That was one of the reasons you hired me in the first place. My experience. With all due respect, you haven't answered my question. Please." I took a deep breath. "I need peace of mind. It's very important for me. Please."

"It has nothing to do with you, so relax. I just feel that I haven't been appreciated enough. We are supposed to be equal. My partner and I." He didn't say 'my partner and friend.' I played this game before. I knew all too well what was the reason he called.

"Look. There's no other way to say this, what I'm about to say." My turn to hit the drama pause button. It's like being at the dentist, and you get a warning about the imminent, unavoidable, and unpleasant pain. "I don't know what's going on between you two. I don't know why, and honestly, I don't want to be dragged into it. You're both my clients. My friends. I see you, and I treat you as one person. I won't take sides, no matter what."

"Then, I guess we're done here. Nothing left to discuss." He didn't try to hide this huge disappointment. I couldn't care less about it.

I was on my way out when his last line grabbed and held me for a moment. "I hope it's understandable that this conversation never took place."

"Absolutely. It's not my job to be a fireman. The last thing I'd do is to pour gasoline on fire between you. Take care. I hope both of you know what you're doing and why."

I was gone.

The Second Co-Founder

"Would you like something to drink? Should we order something?"

"No, I'm good."

Here we go again. I thought to myself—the same scene and motives with a different actor - the other co-founder.

"I hear you've been seeing my partner." They both kept avoiding the word 'friend' like the plague. "Would you mind explaining yourself?"

"Actually, I do mind." The other co-founder didn't expect that I'd be like this. He left me no choice. "Why are you doing this? I don't get you, both of you. You've built something great. Why do you have to be like this, both of you?"

"Did you know it was my family's money that got this whole thing started?" This line sounded familiar. I realized that my work with this startup was over, but their pointless legal battle had just begun.

"Good luck, guys. You're about to ruin something great."

Lots of Loose Ends For Two Former Startup Friends

What happened next with these two co-founders, their company, and most importantly, their app? I did my best to stay out of it. I heard that they had spent more time with their lawyers at the courts than with their employees at the company. The competition took advantage of the situation. They used to be the first and the only app that could do this and that. Now, they're just one of the apps in this category that haven't had an update in years.

Would my contract idea have changed something? I don't think so.

Should they have signed a contract before launching a startup as co-founders? No. Just like with the marriage thing, it's nothing more than a piece of paper.

You keep asking me the wrong questions, so let me save you some time. Here's the right question you should be asking yourself:

Should a startup take off as a single-seat or two-seat fighter jet?

Entrepreneurship Is An Art of Achieving Extraordinary With Ordinary Means

ENTREPRENEURS ALCHEMISTS AND MONEY-MAKING ARTISTS

I grew up hearing that if you want to be the best, you have to invest. Now, when I'm a bit older, and not necessarily wiser, I've had plenty of opportunities to test this claim first-hand.

I remember a client who wanted to sell his app for $150,000. Yet, it was too much for him to pay me $150 for writing a sales letter that he planned to send out to potential investors. So, I said, let's do it for $100. He canceled the project. Later, I found out that he hired another writer to do it for $50. Wow! You want to make $150K, but $150 for a sales letter is too much. Seriously?

Practice What You Teach, If Want To Become Rich

The time has come for me to put my money where my mouth is. So, here I was thinking about whether I should invest $50, $100, or $150 in my first ebook cover professional design. Seriously?

It goes both ways, doesn't it?

You want to catch a whale by using a worm as bait. Then, you have the nerve to ask yourself, what went wrong and why.

My neighbor sells hand-made parts for classic cars. This is a picky and very demanding, but also an extremely rewarding market for skilled people. If there's one thing, the proud owners of classic cars just couldn't care less that is, and it has always been - the price itself. We all love and care about our four-wheel 'pets.' But the classic cars are the next level.

No price is too high. And, the most important thing about classic cars is that you can't just order a missing part. Especially if you are in the middle of your classic car restoration process. I wasn't aware that there's an entire industry built around hand-made parts for classic cars. And, my neighbor was a part of it.

Dream Big - Think Small - Invest Almost Nothing

"Good mornin' neighbor, how's business?"

Literally, every single day, the same old story. I need new machines. I need better tools. I need this. I need that. So, one day, I just had enough.

"OK. Seriously. What's the catch? I like what you're doing. I admire you. For me, you're an artist. I hardly miss a day not visiting you in your garage to see what you're working on."

"It's not that simple."

"Well, the way I see it." I did a 360 spin in his garage. "I don't see computers and robots here. No disrespect, but these are all relatively small and simple tools. We are talking about hand-made products, aren't we?"

"Yes, we are."

"So, how much money do you need to take the next step? Just be honest."

"No more than a thousand dollars, give it or take." His face turned into a meme from 'The Hangover' math (blackjack-card-counting) scene. "Yup, that's about the right amount of money I need."

"But, you don't have that money. Right?" He laughed ironically. That was his answer. "Is that an iPhone you're holding in your hand?"

"Yes, a sure thing it is. I need the top device. This is how I communicate with my clients. The quality of pictures is crucial. I have to be online all the time. I'm working in my garage around the clock. I don't have the time to go up to my apartment and check my computer. That'd be a waste of time."

That was a long story about one phone. Was he trying to justify his 'investment?'

"Is that the latest model? I think I saw the ad." He nodded. "How much does it cost?"

He hesitated. He just couldn't look me in the eye. His iPhone was behind his back. I couldn't believe it. I took my phone and Google it.
"It's almost a thousand dollars. Are you serious?" Good. We identified the problem. "Why don't you sell your phone? Invest in new machines and tools. By the end of this year, you will be able to buy not one but two new iPhones."

"I don't think that's a good idea." He had that 'My Precious' look in his eyes. "I like my iPhone. I'm not going to sell it."

I was seeing red. "Here's my phone. Take it. Use it. When you earn enough to buy a new iPhone again, you can give it back to me."

"That's Samsung. I don't like Samsung phones."

I left his garage. Needless to say, I had been avoiding it for quite some time.

What Happened To 'Give First - Get Later?'

The 'signs' are everywhere. I'm pretty much sure that you can hardly find a single 'Avengers' movie that didn't hit one billion dollars or more at the box office. But, each movie in this franchise had a production and marketing budget of $200M or $300M or even more. My point just couldn't be more obvious, could it?

You can't get something out of nothing. First, you need to invest. I just thought of the Big Bang Theory (not a TV show). My life is too short to get into details, but I have every reason to believe that there was something at the beginning of all beginnings.

We dream crazy dreams about hundreds of thousands of dollars just waiting for us out there. Still, when it comes to taking the first step and investing, we become extremely rational and cautious. I dare to say even - stingy.

It seems that we like to dream big, but when it comes to our pockets (wallets), we think small. I can bet that not much has changed in my neighbor's garage except his phone.

Humble beginnings look cool and inspirational in every entrepreneur's biography. And yes, it's possible from a math and business perspective to earn hundreds or thousands of dollars for every single dollar you invest. But here's the thing. I'm talking about the very first dollar that started the whole thing turning.

The more you give, the more you get. Or, this is some stupid rule you'd be better to forget?

Reciprocity Is The Mother of All Good

I also remember when one client, an enthusiastic startup founder, told me something like: "You will get money when my startup starts making money."

To this very day, I admire myself for being able to continue our conversation in a civilized and respectful tone.

"I apologize, but I think we have a misunderstanding here. If you're looking for a business partner or co-founder, then your plan makes sense. Otherwise, you're asking for free work."

Oh boy, did I bring out this wannabe founder's ugly side? I found myself in the midst of a storm powered by anger and profanity. I lacked the capacity to realize and follow 'the big idea.' I will regret it one day.

"Good. Nice talking to you. Now, find someone else who will be lucky (stupid) enough to buy your story and follow you on your epic journey."

Let me finish that lovely subheading:

RECIPROCITY - The Mother of All Good In Life, Love, and Especially, Especially in Entrepreneurship, period.

*You Can't Be A Kid Forever
And Your Startup
Can't Be A Startup Forever
One Day You Both
Have To Grow Up
and Go Public*

THE STARTUP FOUNTAIN OF YOUTH

Launching a startup is just like writing a book. It's a crazy mixture of excitement and uncertainty.

There aren't too many possible outcomes. Either your startup becomes a company, and your book gets published, or you stop fighting and writing. There's a third option, though. You may leave your book unfinished and your startup undeveloped. It happens. You move on and start building and writing something new.

Did you know that there are 'loopers' among both entrepreneurs and writers? How to recognize one?

It's easier to begin with a writer who's still working on his book. He writes, but never finishes it. I'm still working on it. Time is relative. In a writer's mind (world) who just can't make it to the final chapter, there are only days and weeks. In the outside (real) world, months and years have passed.

It's a bit different in the world of startups, but it eventually comes down to the same outcome. Some founders decide to stay 'forever young.' Their startups are stuck in a 'childhood' phase that's supposed to be temporary - indefinitely. Why?

Can't Stop Dating and Talking About Marrying - At The Same Time

Loopers are cheaters. Admiration without obligation. What are you doing? I'm working on my new book. Wow! That's awesome. I admire you so much. You're so creative. What are you doing? I launched a startup. Wow! You're your own boss now. Kudos! What are you doing? I'm dating someone. Wow! You're so lucky. Fingers crossed. Congrats!

The first couple of times, you can get away with it. You can still come up with some acceptable answers to the same question. However, if you keep hearing the same old question year after year, over and over again, then you have a problem with your book, startup, or relationship.

For five consecutive years, I used to be a come 'n' go freelance writer for one startup. I get a call. I do my job. I get paid. I disappear. Repeat.

I'm not saying that the only measure of success for startups is whether or not they go public one day. There's no stopwatch either. However, one day, you have to make it official. You have to say, we are no longer a startup; we are a company now. Why in the world would you want to delay that moment intentionally?

As a startup, you can never run out of excuses. You can always count on sympathy.

"How's business?"

"It's good. Solid. We're still fighting, but we aren't giving up."

"It has been five years now, if my memory serves me right. We aren't getting any younger."

"What's that supposed to mean?" The Founder looked at me as if we were a couple celebrating an anniversary when a tricky question popped up.

"I mean, aren't you a company already? What more do you need to become one?"

You can tell there's no chance for a win-win when someone is rubbing his chin. "Look, we've known each other for five years. Right. You've been writing for us since day one. That's why I'm going to pretend that you haven't said any of these."

"I meant no disrespect. But what's the catch here? We aren't kids. So, no BS. Please. Five years. I deserved it, didn't I?"

"OK. No BS. Here's the thing." The Founder was warming up for our hard talk episode. "I want to enjoy the feeling a little bit longer. Is there anything wrong about it?"

"What? What feeling? What in the world are you talking about?"

"Launching a startup is dope. You have to do it to understand it."

I needed a couple of minutes to process what I just heard. So, I was sitting across from a business adrenaline junkie. Nothing wrong with it. On the contrary, that's a good thing. But, how about a different approach and solution?

"Why don't you launch another startup? You will feel the same way. Isn't that the easiest and the right thing to do?"

"No. It's not. I don't want to go through all the trouble again. I just want to enjoy this moment."

"Yeah, but this 'moment' has been lasting for five years now."

"For me, it has been like five minutes."

We were silent, for I didn't know how long. Why did I have to bring this transition from a startup to a company thing up? The Founder had been a fair player all these years. It was his thing. Ah, something about the road to hell and my good intentions.

"You just don't understand it. The moment you become a company, everything changes. The magic is gone." He just thought of something. "What's in it for you? Your turn to be totally honest. Don't think about it. Just spit it out."

"For example, I could've been an employee for a couple of years. And, not just me. There's a bunch of guys who could've been full-time employees and not just gigsters who come and go."

"OK. That's a legit point, but it doesn't work for me. Why don't you launch your own startup and see how easy it is to ensure regular work for your people?"

The Founder made his point. I gave him that. Time to change the record because this was obviously a dead-end street.

"So, what do you want me to write about?"

"Now you're talking. Get your laptop. Time to get down to work."

Can't Go Against Fate and An Expiration Date

It was a dry freelance season for me that year. I was going through a list of my old clients. I thought of the Founder. "This number is no longer in service?" What? I usually called. I sent an email. "Mail delivery failed: returning message to sender." What? I tried his startup's website. "This domain is for sale." What's going on? I wasn't the only come 'n' go person the Founder used to work with. I dug some numbers from I didn't know where.

It took some time before I found someone that actually remembered me.

"The Founder has been an old story for some time. Didn't you know what?"

"I have no clue. What happened to him and his startup?"

"Long story short. He'd been hibernating too long. Both investors and gigsters, like you and I, eventually lost their patience. You can't be a startup forever, can't you? Either you grow, or you blow. Shame. He was a good guy, and his startup had potential."

"Do you know what happened to the Founder?"

"The last I heard, he was trying to sell his startup with no success. Nobody was interested in a takeover. I guess, he just got tired and shut it down one day."

"Has he tried to start something new?"

"No, I don't think so. You don't launch a new startup after five years of being a startup. I mean, you can, but still. He could've launched five new startups by now. Each year a new one. At least one of them would've made it. I think."

"I still can't figure out what was he thinking. Even startups have an expiration date."

"You got that one right, buddy. Look, I have to go. Nice talking to you."

The silence of the startup lambs. The Founder got caught in that feeling of his, literally. He lost track of time and everything else.

Has the startup fountain of youth claimed another victim?

No. Did you know that the famous legend about the fountain of youth was all about entrepreneurship? Yup, I did some digging while looking for a nice title for this story. And, I found someone to blame for the whole confusion.

I point the finger at the Pirates of Caribbean franchise. Part four, 'On Stranger Tides,' in particular. Here's why.

The famous fountain of youth researcher, Ponce de León, was an entrepreneur, first and foremost. According to Wikipedia and Woodrow Wilson, Ponce de León was actually looking for a famous aphrodisiac, the so-called 'Bahamian love vine.'

Allegedly, he got lost in a translation. One letter made all the difference. I don't blame him, and neither should you. Instead of 'fountain of vine' ('vid' for vine in native language), he ended up looking for 'fountain of life' ('vida' for life in Spanish).

The rest is history, or it's better to say the legend about the fountain of youth. Sadly, both the Founder in my story and Ponce de León in real life didn't fulfill their entrepreneurship dreams.

What Is Kryptonite To Superman That Is A Big Ego To An Entrepreneur

MY ENTREPRENEUR AMIGO WITH A BIG EGO

There are no humble entrepreneurs, at least, not the successful ones. And, there's nothing wrong or bad about it.

The ego is a beast that hunts and feeds every entrepreneur's self-confidence. The catch is to keep that beast under control all the time. If this is a catch-22 for entrepreneurs, then the following one is a catch-23.

A startup isn't a democracy. It isn't a debate club either. That's why all successful entrepreneurs have the right dosage of autocracy. An entrepreneur has to be a tyrant, but not a full-time tyrant.

Memento Mori, My Dear Entrepreneuori

Think big, or go home. Cheesy, but true. If you don't think highly of yourself, how can you reach the heights of success? Oh dear, this one sounds even worse. Again, sad but true.

I have no intention to lecture you about the history of Ancient Rome. Google it, when you have the time. It's going to be worthy of your time, so find the time to do it. Among many great lessons, just in case, you haven't already heard or read about it, there's one about a slave with a very important role.

This slave was following the Roman emperors around and, with a gentle whisper into their ear, reminded them that even they were mortal. There are variations, 'you are only or just or also a human.'

It goes without saying that this practice was very annoying for Roman emperors. If I were a Caesar (title not a name), I'd send that dude who's breathing down my neck all day long to 'dance with the lions.'

At the same time, this was a life-saving practice. You get carried away, and the next thing you know it, there's a stubbing party with you as the main event. So, it was in your best interest to be reminded to hold your horses of power and ambition from time to time.

As I'm moving to the present time with my story, I have to behave not to get into trouble. What's happening with the modern-time startup Caesars?

The wise ones hire personal assistants to hold them still when they feel a sudden urge to tweet. (DISCLAIMER: I am not implying or comparing the Ancient Rome slaves to the modern-day personal assistants). I plan this to be my final story, so I'm going to allow myself the luxury of letting some steam off.

Nowadays, the Roman emperors wear expensive suits and drive steel chariots 'powered' by hundreds of 'horses.' Good luck if you try to get close enough to whisper something into their ear.

Because of the whole COVID situation, we all have to attend virtual meetings and conference calls. I honestly don't see a big difference from a strictly business perspective. You may be out of a virus reach, but it doesn't mean you're out of your startup emperor's reach.

It was one of those regular meetings. I think we were using Zoom or was it Skype? It doesn't matter. One of the lead developers had a civilized conversation with a startup's founder and CEO (Cyber Caesar) by any business standards. He threw out some ideas for improving the overall functionality and efficiency. He had an episode of honest, constructive criticism, but nothing serious or disrespectful.

I did my very best to notice if some eyebrows were raised during his presentation, but I ran into technical difficulties. Either the faces of people attending looked too small on my screen, or not all of them had their cameras turned on. Everybody said what needed to be said and asked what needed to be asked. The next meeting was scheduled for the beginning of the following month.

Your Royal Startup Highness, You Are Full of Madness

The next meeting got the whole together—all team members, except one. The lead developer with a big mouth (?!) wasn't present. I minded my own business until the meeting was officially over. Then, I tried to ask around in our virtual working space what happened to him and why.

Usually, when someone wasn't present at our meetings, we got a notification and an explanation. This was different and strange. It became even more awkward while I was trying to find out more about the MIA developer. What kind of a 'digital omerta' was this? How did we come to this, our own code of silence?

All I could get in return were some ambiguous answers and 'friendly pieces of advice,' such as, 'better not to ask,' 'it's for your own good,' 'what is it to you,' and similar cyber BS. I got the message. I had to read between the lines. A team member was removed, and we were pretending as if he never existed and worked with us.

OK. If it had to be this way, let it be. I could only guess what happened between the developer and Cyber Caesar from the last meeting. Honestly, I didn't have the time to play this guessing game. I had my own work to do.

But, the disappearance trend didn't end with one of the startup's lead developers. One week, you just found out that one of the designers was removed from your working group. Some other week, you get a simple and heartless email that you were to work with a new guy on marketing tasks from now on.

Did we just go through our startup's version of The Purge movie? There was no way for me to confirm or discuss my doubts. Everywhere I tried to get additional information, I'd only hit the wall of silence. The pattern was too obvious to ignore. The consequences were quick and effective, not to be acknowledged. There's a thin line between corporatism and individualism. But hey, we were a startup. We were supposed to be unconstrained and creative. We were explorers, not soldiers.

One day there were just too many new faces to play dumb and look the other way. In my humble opinion, anyone with the minimum capacity for critical reasoning and constructive criticism was gone. I knew my place all too well. If we were to set on a journey to Marks, a writer wouldn't be treated as a part of the mission-critical personnel in any movie.

But, my startup baby, I have only one life to live and a limited number of productive years to give. So, let me see for myself what was happening with our startup emperor's new groove and what he was planning for his next move.

"Hi there. It's nice to see and hear you. We don't talk too often, you and I." Cyber Caesar was available for a call. I didn't have to give a reason why. He was super cool and friendly. I decided to have a conversation without prejudices. What do I know of what has been happening in our startup backstage?

"I only talk when I have something important to say."

"I love that about you. For a writer, you ain't much of a talker. You do your work. People around here respect you and don't complain about you." We were still in the friendly zone. Maybe this was his way of expressing satisfaction with someone's work. Interesting choice of words, though. "So, is there something I can help you with? Do you need something?"

It's showtime! "I couldn't help noticing that we have made quite a few personal changes recently." I worked on my intro, but Cyber Caesar made sure I didn't have to use it.

"First, we didn't do a thing. I made all these changes. Second, why should you be worried about it?"

"I'm not worrying. I'm just asking." Video calls are no match for meetings in person, but they still have their advantages. Without the distractions of the outside real world, you can focus all of your attention on even the slightest changes of facial expressions and tone of voice.

My personal interpretation of what I just heard was a bit different. 'Oh, I didn't know you were one of those, I had to get rid of. So, let me remind you who I am. I gave you a chance to back down, but you wanted to ask questions.'

"I see no point in wasting your breath on asking questions that don't concern you, not even remotely."

Oh, baby, I love it when you talk dirty to me. "I'm investing my time here."

"I'm investing my money here." Oh, that was a nice return of my serve. Time to feel the power of his forehand return. "I call the shots here. I don't have to explain myself. We ain't a democracy."

"True. But, I see no need to become an autocracy either."

"You'd be surprised how things quickly escalate to a complete anarchy without an iron fist."

"Oh, how did we reach a point where we have to bring iron fists into our conversation?"

"Cut to the chase! I don't have time for this. Unlike you, I'm investing both my time and money. Right now, nobody is paying me to answer your pointless questions."

Startup Nodders vs. Startup Believers

"Startups can afford to lose countless employees and investors. People come. People go. But to lose one true believer is one too many."

"Wow! You're a writer, alright." Cyber Caesar laughed. "There's just one part I don't get. Who are those true believers? Are you one of them?"

"I used to be, but then I realized something. If you want people to work for you, you fill their wallets. But if you want them to bleed for you, you need to fill their hearts too."

Cyber Caesar's face filled the whole screen. "I don't need believers. I need soldiers. May I share my favorite quote with you?" His question hit the silence. "Please indulge me." Cyber Caesar was using the word 'please.' It had to be good. I nodded.

"Have you seen the movie 'Runner Runner' with Ben Affleck and Justin Timberlake?"

"It rings a bell. Something about online gambling, if I'm not mistaken."

"Yeah, that's the one. Ben Affleck outperformed himself in that movie. Wouldn't you agree?"

I wanted to mention 'Argo,' but this wasn't a movie night. "Please return a favor. Your turn to cut to the chase."

"Please give me a second. It's more than one line." He could see that I was rolling my eyes. "Don't be like that. I promise, it's going to be worth remembering. Ah, here it is. Ready?" One more nod to a self-proclaimed business god.

"Oh boy, this is priceless. You must've missed or you didn't pay attention. Here it goes. *'This is your job. You want a clear conscience, go start a charity. But if you want your own island and your boss says you gotta go out there and take a beating, you go out there, take it and come back to work and say, do you need me to do it again?'* The character in this movie has stolen these beautiful words right out of my mouth and heart."

"You must've seen this movie more than once." Cyber Caesar nodded. "Then, you clearly remember how the movie ended, don't you?"

"Yup. The boss in that movie got played and betrayed. It ain't gonna happen to me. Those so-called 'believers' you admire so much are all potential 'traitors.' You don't bite a hand that feeds you and your family. You don't question my authority in front of the whole team, period."

His cheek was resting on his hand covering the closed fist.

"That's why you will always be surrounded by nodders. They may be good at following and obeying, but I'm afraid they suck when it comes to creating new things and contributing with new ideas."

"If you're so smart and you think you know better, why don't you launch your own startup and tell me how it goes?"

"Memento Mori, My Dear Entrepreneuori."

"What was that? Sorry, no parlo Italiano." His laughter pushed my headphones membrane to the limit.

"All the best, Sir."

"Put this in one of your stories."

Call ended.

ABOUT THE AUTHOR

Nebojsa Nesha Todorovic

I smoke like Mark Twain.
I drink like Ernest Hemingway.
I kiss like Charles Bukowski.
I write like myself.

www.ingramcontent.com/pod-product-compliance
Lightning Source LLC
Chambersburg PA
CBHW070419220526
45466CB00004B/1463